Friendly Musings

FORWORD

I was milling around the meeting courtyard, as Friends often do at the rise of meeting on sunny afternoons, when Friend Lee approached me. Crossing paths may have been random, but what Lee said to me was too odd for that. "We should write down messages from meeting," she quipped, completely out of the blue. No message from the Spirit could have been clearer than that.

I thought it was a good idea. After all, Downingtown Friends has been blessed with rich vocal ministry and a vibrant spiritual life. Social media was nonexistent back then, but I have always felt that the Spirit speaks to everybody, and its message should be heard beyond the walls of the meeting house. Without a distinct plan in mind, *Friendly Musings* was born.

Some twenty years went by, and just as I began seeking clearness about the scope of the project, this query was read in meeting: "Does meeting ministry lead Friends to share their spiritual experiences with others? Are we tender to the needs of others in need of spiritual support?"

It was another not-so-random prompting. Even if the divine dimension of worship cannot be replicated, *Friendly Musings* might just be the answer, I thought.

The vocal ministry presented here has resonated with me the most. Much like the Friends in meeting who shaped me by living their beliefs, these messages have been key to my spiritual growth. Interspersed, the reader will find gleanings from various adjunct programs in meeting.

I am much indebted to Friend Lee for her leading and to all the other Friends for their feedback and support. I am overjoyed to share this Light of the Spirit.

*   *

Quakers, known as Friends, are members of the Religious Society of Friends. Friends worship in meetings—the equivalent of a local church. Eastern Pennsylvania is home to over one hundred such meetings, and their umbrella organization is Philadelphia Yearly Meeting—PYM. PYM saw its beginning in 1682 when William Penn founded a Quaker Colony, later named Pennsylvania.

Unlike some other Quakers groups, PYM meetings have no ministers, sermons, or set ceremonies for service. Worship takes places in silence. Friends may be moved to rise and share a divinely inspired message called vocal ministry.

Vocal ministry is not recorded in worship. Any revelation in the course of such worship dissipates at the end of that session. By capturing a slice of Downingtown Friends spiritual life, *Friendly Musings* may fill a small piece of that void. It may give the reader a sense of what transpires in Friends worship and in a Quaker meeting at large.

Alex Miller
Downingtown Friends Meeting
Downingtown, PA 2016

MEETING FOR WORSHIP

Meeting for worship is best understood in terms of "worthship," that is, intense focus on that which is the dearest to one's heart. Friends gather in silence in the presence of the divine Light. They center to still their minds and hearts and thus open to the voice of the Spirit.

Out of silence, a Friend may be moved to share an inspired message. It may be a thought or a prayer, a reading, or even a song. Messages often speak to the condition of others, lending guidance to their worship.

In worship, Friends may give thanks to the good in their lives and connect with good in all people, consider service to others or simply rejoice in the glory of God's Creation. Worship may be a time to revisit past experiences for better answers or a time to steer challenges in one's life toward the Light.

Worship doesn't start or end at the meeting doors. Friends prepare for it throughout the week in prayer, reflection, and with inspirational fountains. Corporate worship creates a sacred space where Friends share the Light-inspired wisdom.

In Quaker speech, "Walking in the Light" implies incessant search for the truth and witness to the world.

Musings

A SUNRISE ON MOUNT FUJI

Drew's take on love

I was on a business trip in Japan some fifty years ago. My host claimed that no one can visit Tokyo without seeing a sunrise on Mount Fuji.

So, one morning we woke at three o'clock and trekked half way through Tokyo to a point where Mount Fuji can be seen.

As dawn broke, the mountain was engulfed in mist, and when the sun finally came up, the entire horizon became a hazy glob.

In light of the taxing nocturnal adventure, I expressed some disappointment. My host smiled and gently opined: "This is the way we—the Japanese—like to see it." Sensing my confusion, he added gently: "We like it this way for it resembles life where nothing is ever clear."

Apostle Paul laid out the three virtues: Faith, Hope, and Love.

The first two of these are hazy, much alike the mystery-shrouded sunrise on Mount Fuji.

We can hope that our dreams come true, and we can have unwavering faith in the future. There is no absolute certainty, however, that either will materialize.

On the other hand, having been in love with my wife for sixty-five years, I can say with certainty that of the three, the love amongst us is the only virtue that is definite and real.

ROOM IN THE HEART

Jane's take on love

When Gene and I were dating, we were very happy.

We felt our hearts were full of love.

And at our wedding, we were so excited we felt that now our hearts were filled with love.

Then our children were born. We were a family, and with each one, we felt that *now* our hearts were filled with love.

We then joined meeting. We met wonderful Friends and made wonderful friends.

We have achieved spiritual fulfillment and thought that now… our hearts were really filled with love.

Then… our grandchildren were born, and the cycle of life began again. We felt this was the time for more love in our hearts.

And now, as our youngest daughter is getting married, we once again feel more love entering our hearts.

In fact, no matter how much love one has, there is always more room in the heart.

That is the human condition.

You can never totally fill up your heart with love because the more love you put in there, the bigger the space for love gets.

SAM OF LIGHT

The Light of God is in everyone, Friends say.

I found that Light in Sam, the mentally challenged father whose life story is the theme of the film titled *I am Sam*.

I was deeply touched by the Light shining so powerfully in Sam the person and the parent.

Sam had no special skill or parenting experience. His love was natural, unbound, and effortless.

In fact, Sam's only asset was his Light—his intuition.

The Light is innate

The Light must be cherished

The Light must be trusted

The Light is not indestructible

The Light can fade and become dull

It happened to Sam's attorney

She—the other parent in the film—was intelligent, well educated, and professionally highly successful.

Her highly valued personal assets, however, became a hindrance to her Light and to her parental intuition.

In stark contrast with Sam's success as a parent, the attorney's relationship with her son was utterly frustrating to her and disastrous to the son.

A PHONE CONVERSATION

For a number of years, I was out of town two days a week. On those nights, I would call my daughter on the phone for a "tuck-me-in" session.

One such phone conversation took an abrupt turn: "Are you afraid of dying?" she asked. She was nine-years old at the time.

Instinctively, I offered a cliché from a Chinese movie:

"No, I said, because you are me, and because I am you. So when I die, I am really not dead!"

"Where do you go when you die?" she continued.

"Heaven…?" I probed cautiously.

"Is that really true?" she went on with the grilling.

I tried next the "Heaven is here and now" line:

"I believe that if I am nice to you, you will love me, and I will be in Heaven; and if I am not nice to you, you will hate me, and I will be in Hell."

The ensuing pause left me in the dark as far as having passed the test.

She finally said, "Ah Dad, let's be quiet for a minute so I can feel your presence." My daughter was raised in meeting and had heard plenty of Quaker talk. Still, her last comment left me reeling. I was simply floored.

Children's spiritual acuity cannot be overstated.

PO CEGDA

Po cegda budyet sontze
Po cegda budyet nyeba
Po cegda budyet mama
Po cegda budu ya

In this song, a cheerful young girl sings praise for all the reassuring permanence in her life:

Forever is the sun
Forever is the sky
Mama is forever
I am forever

Spiritually, we, as the girl in the song, are the sum-total of certain building blocks. We are collages of people, places, and life experiences. The permanence of those building blocks is what gives us the safety to grow and the wherewithal to thrive.

I felt that truth most intensely with the passing of my father. His death closed a window in my horizon, leaving a void and darkness. A piece of the collage that was me disappeared forever.

At the same time, though, I came to realize a fact of equal importance.

In a broad sense, while we are collages made of others, we are also components in other people's make-up. We are part and parcel of their own collages.

Whether we recognize it or not, by virtue of our existence, we play a fundamental role in someone else's permanence. No matter how marginal we are to their lives, no matter how little we influence their universe, to them, our very existence has great spiritual importance.

THE SIMPLE SAGE

A sage sat with his disciples

He handed a velvet pouch to the first
Fill this copper vessel, he said

The disciple took the rocks from the pouch and
Filled the vessel

The sage smiled, and pulled out a second pouch
The next disciple poured the gravel from it and
Filled the vessel

The sage took yet another pouch
The third disciple poured sand into the vessel
Until the vessel was full

The sage then poured water
into the copper vessel soaking the sand
Now the vessel is full, he said

*   *

The vessel is your life
The rocks are God
The rest are duties and possessions and clutter

Fill your life with God first and
You will have a full life

Change the order and
Your life will be nothing but
Duties and possessions and clutter

Quaker simplicity at its best!

WHO NEEDS GOD

Once upon a time, lightning, thunder, and earthquakes were terrifying signs from Heavens. Disease and death were omens from above.

Man ascribed the domain over his existence entirely to the mercy of God.

As science unraveled the mysteries of nature and technology lifted humanity from the brink of existence, man began reclaiming that domain for himself.

In one nanosecond of Creation, God became irrelevant, and man assumed full control over his destiny and his world.

Emboldened by his triumphs, man embarked on a mindless and increasingly daring conquest of uncharted terrain. No parachute had been contemplated.

In his arrogance and haste, man upended the age-old balance of the Earth—the foundation of his very existence.

He dismissed God's eons-old stasis of life. Instead, man deified himself by creating his own version of it.

Within man's unfettered adventures are the means fit to obliterate God's Creation altogether.

Man is more in danger than ever before. He is now at the mercy of new unpredictable forces well surpassing his first nemeses.

Nunc concipitur mali hominis crimen

GOD'S TREE OF KNOWLEDGE

Of all biblical tales, the story of the Tree of Knowledge may be the most perplexing and significant at the same time.

God had been extremely generous to allow man access to *all* of His Creation. He had set one limit—a symbolic one perhaps—to what is man's and what is His.

The fable is as relevant today as ever, for man has relentlessly and indiscriminately pursued knowledge, without pause to question whether he may have reached God's limit.

Over time, man played engineer, harnessing more and more of God's world for himself. He played scientist, unraveling the mysteries that once had terrified him—the earthquakes, the volcanoes, and the raging storms.

He found earthly causes to explain them and tools to predict them. Man played doctor and defeated the diseases that had once wiped out populations.

Despite all his achievements, man has not created anything himself. All he has done was to play with God's Creation. For that he did get God's blessing.

And then, man discovered the knowledge that enables him to create life on his own. He discovered the book of life known only to God.

Was that the Tree of Knowledge forbidden by God? What will man's trespass lead to? The allegory says man was expelled from a biblical Eden. It could be the real one next.

SPACE FROM SILENCE

Friends worship in silence.

To an outsider, it may seem as if Friends just sit and do nothing. At times, that is probably true. They may even fall asleep on occasion.

But as a Friend once said, we don't just sit in silence worshipping as individuals; we create a sacred spiritual space. It is the space that invites the divine Spirit to be among us.

As precious as that space may be, Friends often struggle to carry it with them beyond the confines of worship.

In daily exchange between Friends, a simple "Greetings to you, Friend" would suffice, but we ask "How are you?" instead and hope not to find out. Simply put, we don't have the space for it.

Space is the best gift one can ever give. It is a token of genuine interest in one's person and the cement of all relationships. Yet, we routinely shortchange our friends and Friends, our families, and our children.

Children may ignore a passing offense, but in the long run, it is the children who are impaired the most. An ill-timed offense of a child asks to be remedied at once.

A long time ago, I had a friend named Zack. I often wondered what it was about Zack that made him a great friend.

Now I know. It was Zack's ability to always avail his friendly space. With Zack, I always felt genuinely loved.

9

SUCCESS AND FAILURE

One day, my daughter showed me her high school yearbook. *My* school couldn't afford yearbooks, and so it was my very first time seeing one. I examined it with care. The achievements section with "the most musical," "the best dressed," and "the best in sports" ended with the "most likely to succeed."

I asked myself what is success? And how could the yearbook predict it with such ease? Fame and riches are common measures of success. Some success gurus expand the scope to be the best person you can be—a volunteer, a successful parent, or a family provider.

*   *

The commencement speaker at my daughter's graduation said: "Fortunate are those few who can find a purpose larger than themselves to affect the greater good." That departure from material possessions takes success into the spiritual realm. My daughter may be a fortunate one, for she did find in music her conduit to inspire others.

But why should one depend on others to set their bar for success? And finally, I realized that success is nothing but the opposite of failure! Set your own goals. If you achieve them, you succeeded. If not, you failed. Should the success scouts look for seniors with realistic goals?

Success takes sacrifice, but its price is rarely talked about. Success that compromises one's integrity and personal values, success that sacrifices relationships or one's spiritual life, success that entails selling one's soul is not the kind of success I seek for myself or advise to others.

ABSTRACT ART

My ten-year-old daughter suggested that we look at an Art Encyclopedia together.

A plate depicting a series of overlapping red squares captured her attention. "What's this?" she said, "Why is this art?"

The caption in the book was no help, for it wasn't much better than what I could come up with.

But two things *can* be said about abstract art. One, it does raise questions. And two, it invites the viewers' own unique insights.

Abstract art is much like Quakerism, for Quakerism enables each and every one their own unique path to the truth and to the Light.

Quakerism is by no means an easy task. It takes self-reliance and discipline. It takes faith in continuing revelation and in the power of the Spirit. No doubt, it can be mighty frustrating at times.

It can also be a great experience. My ten-year journey at Downingtown Meeting has been the source of great spiritual growth.

I feel more centered and empowered, more clear-minded and determined. My spiritual journey led me to connect with my Inner Light and to listen to the leadings of the Spirit.

I am more empathetic and forgiving. I feel I am a better spouse, parent, and person.

PEACE & LOVE—THE SOUL OF CHRISTMAS

"On the doorsteps of year 2000 we may reflect on our lives. Have we embraced peace and love in all our endeavors?

In the wake of turbulence, unrest, and the tormenting realities of everyday life, it is crucial that Light should lead us back to the most sacred of human feelings.

The celebration of Christmas has reminded us for two-thousand years that nothing surpasses the importance of peace and tranquility. The happiness of our families is at their foundation.

When our star pales and the focus on them becomes a challenge, Christmas is the Light to guide us home. As we gather with our loved ones, let us keep in our hearts those who are alone and far away.

Let the scent of the pine in our home remind us of that which, for at least another two thousand years, will be mankind's staunchest ally anywhere—love and peace. Merry Christmas!"

These poetic and inspiring words traveled five thousand miles to reach us. They belong to the mayor of a muddy little village at the foothills of the Carpathian Mountains— a village in a communist country, not long ago.

They could easily be the words spoken right here in our midst; right here in our meeting. They are living proof that the Light of God is in everyone.

They are living proof that people everywhere desire one and the same thing: To live their lives in peace and love.

12

OUR TIME

In modern times, time is everything.

Our lives are driven by time. Speed and productivity power our economy. It is hard to imagine life without the constraint of time.

In retirement, having escaped the yoke of time, I felt great relief. I felt I could rebel; that I could exact a drop of revenge for the long rat race in which I had been a willing participant.

I took on an elaborate landscaping project in my backyard. I felt a grain of bemusement. I set my mind to do everything slowly and inefficiently. For a while, it was actually fun.

I thought of the basket-making monks who dismantled their unsold products at the end of market day.

Time was no longer an issue, but oddly, after some time, I found myself rushing to complete particular phases of the landscaping job.

Bringing a particular task to completion seemed to matter more than the presence in the process.

And no, I could not see myself dismantling anything that I had already done.

Am I having a time-addiction relapse?

Must I relinquish all my goals?

Must I be a monk?

OUR TIME IN THE WORLD

Our time on Earth; what is it for? Most of it isn't ours. We pay our dues to society by earning a living, to our bodies in nourishment and rest, and to our dependents by provision and guidance.

Once in a while, after all that is accomplished, there is time left to spare. What do we do with it? What is there to be done with it?

I asked a friend who was well past most of those obligations: "What have you been doing, John?" "I've been going crazy," he replied in frustration.

That may be the exact reason why some people dread free time and prefer to spend their days at a dulling job that they don't need to do.

In my own struggle with time, a grain of wisdom captured my imagination: People have the moral calling to make the world a better place.

"Better" is limited only by one's ambitions and imagination, for better is on the path to perfection—the elusive goal never to be reached.

Perfection applies to a home and to a garden, to family and to friendship, to a job, a town, or perhaps even to a peaceful utopian world.

The place to start is oneself

There is no limit to learning

There is no limit to what can be taught and shared

A RECIPE FOR ETHICS

A wise man asked me: "If my best friend confesses to committing murder, would I, out of loyalty, keep the secret or call the authorities?"

Tough question! Even tougher if the act had yet to be committed.

Ethical quandaries large and small are everywhere, and in due time, we will all encounter one.

Many years ago, a colleague of mine committed, in my presence, an appalling act. Unlike many events of life that reside in the gray area, this one was pitch black.

Instead of doing something about it, I stood by conveniently shocked. Rather than standing up, I stood by. I know now that I missed a great opportunity to do the "right thing."

Subsequently, I spent years running scenarios through my mind, spinning various actions I could have taken. Everything was better than standing by and do nothing. Strange penance!

Supplementing family and schools, a faith community is and should be the anchor for ethical awareness.

Ethical quandaries large and small are everywhere. Sooner or later we will all encounter one. Ethics alone will not suffice to face off the morally challenging situations. It takes courage, but it also takes preparation.

Will we be ready? Will we stand up or stand by as I had done?

FROM THE BOOK

Quakers rarely talk about the Old Testament. Its perennial violence is antithesis to the peace testimony.

It seems as if human life in biblical times had no value. Public stoning was the norm. Lifting a twig on the Sabbath was punishable by death.

In Isaac's story, human sacrifice is contemplated. To us, a bound-up child laid on the altar of sacrifice by his own father is unfathomable.

But "thou shall not kill" is not about the sanctity of life as seen today. Its "thou shall not murder" progenitor was strictly a matter of law and order.

The Old-Testament God's license for violence is disturbing.

The biblical Hebrews were told to crush tribes, destroy their cities, and kill every soul and all livestock.

How can Quakers profess pacifism and preach the Bible at the same time?

*   *

The specter of violence may have just been the
lightning rod of awakening

Is the Old Testament a memorial for what
must never happen again?

Would you expect a peace testimony
to emerge in a peaceful place?

16

WHAT IS GOD'S WIILL?

Are we able to know?

The holy books are words of God

They may contradict others' holy books

And there are Quakers who don't go by the book

If God is beyond human comprehension,
how can He possibly convey His will to us?

Is God's will the same for all people?

Is God's will just for people or for all His creatures?

Does the Almighty God
really need or want anything from us lowly humans?

Is there anything to be sure of?

We do exist
The Universe around us exists
It is God's Creation

God's will must be his Creation

Live it
Guard it
Perpetuate it
Or just BE

17

A LETTER TO A YOUNG FRIEND

Dear Sylvia,

This is to thank you and to commend you for your message on Easter Sunday.

It was the best message I have heard in a long time.

I felt it was the epitome of everything that has happened in meeting in the last twenty-five years—all the worship meetings and vocal ministry, the Opening Exercises, and all the formal events and the social chit-chat.

It was especially gratifying for me to see that you have blossomed into a charismatic and confident spiritual adult.

I fantasize about the day when my own daughter will stand up where you stood and deliver an encore.

I hope your message will prove to be just one of many to come!

Thank you again, and all the best to you!

In peace,

Your friend and Friend

WHAT'S IN A PHRASE?

Words can be exasperating.

Of all the many, only a particular one, at a particular time will hit home.

What can be more formidable than comprehending God?

Captions such as "Universal Consciousness" and "We are all One," "Pure Consciousness" and "Cosmic Energy" attempt to convey what the Spirit of God might be.

Over the years, I have heard them all and many others. They meant nothing to me.

They added nothing to my feeble grasp of the Universe and my place it.

Then came this: "You are the result of everything that ever happened in the Universe."

It is an obvious and undeniable truth.

Without galactic explosions, there would be no sun or life on Earth, no human existence, and no me.

As simple as it was, that phrase was my epiphany.

I felt no longer disjointed and adrift

I felt infinite and invincible as the Universe

I felt empowered and perfected

I felt simplicity, balance, and joy

OF GOD AND COMPUTERS

You can talk to computers now. Typing mavens can bang out words on the keyboard faster than that and, with the mouse, anyone can zip to their heart's desire.

The color screen and hi-fi speakers let you see, hear, and know all you want to know.

None of them have a thing to do with computing. Remove them, and the mind-boggling chain of zeros and ones will go on.

They are merely accessories invented by very smart people to allow a glimpse inside the madness.

Like the digital storm in the machine, the essence of God is beyond human grasp. It was not crafted by mortals. No monitors or speakers exist.

Once in a while, a guide may emerge who by virtue of contemplation or divine gift might bring forth a link to that universal truth.

Is the Scripture a venue to that end? Are the angels the speakers? Are the rituals the keyboard, and the Creation around us the color screen?

I would like to believe that. I would like to believe that the biblical parables are mere allegories meant to shed light onto the truth.

Perhaps words like "king," "blood," and "father and son" were strictly metaphors—the only words people understood in those times. They may have been ancient computer peripherals.

THE NEIGHBOR'S GRASS

The grass is always greener on the other side. So they say. It sure looked that way from my porch! I was well aware that the "greener grass" was about the human condition and not about grass, but still…

So, one day, while my neighbors weren't around, I quickly snuck over to their yard. I simply had to put my mind to rest.

Lo and behold! The neighbors' grass *was* greener! And then, it became quite clear. It hadn't been a matter of a cliché; I just wasn't nursing my lawn the way my neighbor did.

Clichés are great, but how can the metaphoric grass be greener or better on the other side when there is that of God in everyone?

The greener-grass illusion is a powerful fact of life

If allowed to overpower our vision, the greener grass
will lead us into the pursuit of imaginary ideals

If allowed to overpower our vision, the greener grass
will lead us into frustration and consume us with jealousy

If allowed to overpower our vision, the greener grass
will lead us to devalue all that is dear in our existence

Why is that?

I could start guessing

But I will leave it for all to ponder

DAVID'S CALLING

The Philistines and the Israelites had been locked in a thirty-day stand-off. No Hebrew had dared to answer Goliath's challenge for a one-to-one fight to decide the outcome of the battle.

That changed when the seventeen-year-old David came to camp with food for his brethren. While there, David received a divine leading that he could defeat the Philistine hero.

Eliab, David's eldest brother and head of camp, wanted no part of it. He worried that David would be killed, the Hebrews would lose the battle, and that his family would be shamed. "Go home David, tend Father's flock!" Eliab said.

Eliab acted as a protective older brother would, out of concern for David's well-being and the fate of his people. He knew nothing of David's divine calling. As is always the case, David alone knew! It was David's destiny.

You are in Eliab's shoes
Your brother, sister, or child is moved by a calling

What right do you have
to prevent them from fulfilling their destiny?

What right do you have
to live your children's lives for them?

Where would you stop in protecting your child?

How would you know when
the risk outweighed their calling?

WHY SIMPLICITY

I grew up in a small yellow house

It had two rooms, a kitchen, and a pantry called "speitz"

The water and the potty were out in the yard

Electricity came when I was ten

I had a few toys, a chess-set, and an occasional cat

I spent great a deal of my time
with my mom and with my thoughts

I mastered every trick about my toys
I knew every detail in the house and
every inch of the yard and the attic

I got a solid foundation in the basics of life
self-reliance, clarity of thought, intuition

I acquired intense curiosity and
a voracious hunger for knowledge

I thought that having all the luxuries we have today would have been better. They would have made me a better person. There may be a bit of truth to that.

But the head fills up quickly. Attention span only goes so far. Hasty knowledge that cannot be sensibly stored and retrieved is useless junk.

Once the head is full, curiosity and common sense go away. The Spirit is simply crowded out.

A PERSONAL JOURNEY

After college, I embarked on a low-budget, ten-country trip to Europe. I visited famous tourist icons from the Westminster Abbey in London to the Acropolis in Athens.

I bumped into Amsterdam's seven-hundredth jubilee, a Dutch cat exposing its tongue, and an eight-foot giant in London's Kew Gardens. I witnessed a middle-age Serb shedding a river of tears, a beggar on Trafalgar square who looked like an aristocrat, and two professional drunkards hanging out in Vienna.

Others may have seen them too, but no one has seen all of them, and no one interpreted them exactly the way I did. It had been *my* journey. They have become *my* experience.

Spiritual journeys are much like the real life one.

We have springs of wisdom as the Scriptures and the Inner Light. Random gems surface unexpectedly. We learn from each other. We encounter people, landmarks, and experiences. Some are uplifting, others are dull. Their synthesis gives birth to our spiritual journey.

Expecting only inspiring encounters would not only be unrealistic but futile.

Unless you would rather adopt someone's pre-packaged spirituality, expecting all vocal ministry in meeting to speak to your condition makes no sense.

Sorting out what does and what doesn't may just be the whole point of the journey.

A VISIT TO LONDON

London was the first stop of my European trip. The year was 1975, and I was twenty-five years old. I had spent my young-adult life in a closed-in, stress-laden, chaotic land, where disregard for civility was a sport and information a luxury.

My first day in London happened to be the day when the Westminster Abbey was open to the public. Needless to say, its splendor was beyond words. Other marvels followed: the palaces at Buckingham and Windsor, the Wax Museum, and Saint Paul's Cathedral.

Millions see these sites and bathe in their grandeur, but *my* fascination quickly wore off. My mind was captivated by impressions that eluded most tourists or bore no significance to them. Those are still fresh in my mind.

The greatest miracle were London's commuters. There were no railings at the bus stop or markings on the ground, yet people formed long double-width perfect lines to get on. To me, it was a mirage I couldn't get enough of. Even though tremendously self-conscious, I watched riveted from a distance until the bus arrived.

I passed a young father holding a shopping bag in one hand and the hand of his five-year-old son with the other. They were engaged in a joyous exchange and were clearly very proud of each other.

It was picture-perfect harmony, something *I* really wanted. In fact, I was so taken by the scene that, ignoring all etiquette and embarrassment, I whipped out my black-and-white camera, turned around and took a shot. Nobody noticed.

A MORNING IN THE GARDEN

A fresh spring morning found me on the veranda of a bed and breakfast in Larnaca on the coast of Cyprus. The year was 1978. Most of the guests were well-to-do Lebanese fleeing the civil war flaring up in their country.

Facing the veranda was a small rose garden enclosed by blooming oleander and colorful bougainvillea.

A somber man stood in the garden, oblivious to the people around him, in trance-like communion with the solace of his mini paradise.

In his late seventies, he had short white hair and the build of a mountain. He was the proprietor. That was as obvious as the burdens of life etched in his stone-like face. Had he been a guerilla fighter, a commander in island's own civil war, or just witness to untold misery in his lifetime?

He wasn't checking on employees, schmoozing the guests, or sitting in his office doing the books. But his presence in the garden added distinct spiritual dimension to the place.

We need heroes and role models, and this man certainly was one for me. He gave me an unforgettable gift. His figure and aura are still with me as they were thirty years before. How exactly has that sunny Cypriot morning affected my life, I will, of course, never know.

I hope, though, that this great man can look down upon me from wherever he now is. I hope he can see himself in my incarnation, moving in slow-motion in my garden, day after day, emulating the stillness of his mind and his presence in the Spirit.

THE POWER OF PRESENCE

A visibly distraught young man wanders in the city crowd, saddled with a life decision. A street-corner preacher notices his concern and whispers: "Son, there are signs everywhere."

Taken aback at first by the comment, the young man begins to notice all the signs that seem to be addressed directly to him.

*　　*

Meeting for worship is a time to center into the Spirit, to let go of concerns, and to listen for signs from the Divine.

That awareness need not stop at the meeting house doors. Ministry is everywhere. There is ministry in presence only.

*　　*

Our routine walk had been completely silent. My walking partner—my wife—seemed sullen. I asked her if she was upset with me.

"No," she replied, "but why?"

"You hadn't said a word to me."

"I still enjoyed your presence."

E-mail* is a great conduit to ministry. I exchange several messages with my daughter every day.

At times it is a sentence, often—a word only. I then carry her presence the whole day. I feel connected as I do in worship.

*pre-Facebook days

HOW YOU ARRIVE

Two men lie on the beach basking in the morning sun. Gentle surf laps the dunes. Seagulls circle above.

No trace remains of the storm the night before.

One man had just walked down from his beach-house to catch a few rays. He dozed off contemplating his great life and his wonderful vacation.

The other man seems to be asleep too. He may actually be unconscious. He is a washed-up survivor from a fishing boat shipwrecked in the night's storm.

Two men are on a sunny beach. They are at the same place at the same time but had arrived there in very different ways.

"The journey is more important than the destination," they say. Coaches stress to players that playing the game right is more important than winning.

Once reached, the peak of the mountain loses appeal. The luster of the material world fades once the top is reached. Possessions become dull and boring. What you are left with are the memories of how you got there.

Memories matter, for they have tenacious powers. They sneak into the psyche and hijack your thoughts. They even rule your dreams. And they never ever go away.

A joyful spiritual journey is paved with joyful memories.

Laughter Ministry Smiles Breakthroughs Love
Comradery Spirit Excitement Music Revelation

VISION AND PROVISION

The movie *Amadeus* is about the genius of Amadeus Mozart and the ambitions of his nemesis—Antonio Salieri. Salieri had vowed to devote his life and soul to serve God through the glory of music and had been rewarded by fame and success as a court composer.

His blind jealousy of Mozart, however, leads him to believe that it was the hand of God that kept him from being the best; from being Mozart. In his anger he turns to God: "Why implant the desire and then deny the talent?"

Even if moved by the strongest of desires, we cannot all be Mozart. Friends are moved to action by the God-planted Inner Light. They and others have followed that Light to great ends. One needs to go no further than Gandhi or Jesus to see how millions have been touched.

I feel blessed for the many desires I have had. True, I haven't always followed them through.

The task is often daunting. Obstacles dampen the Spirit. Doubt and insecurity arise. One might even feel selfish to indulge in the pursuit of a personal ambition.

But the leadings of the Spirit are not private desires. They are divinely planted seeds.

Once you take action, others will get behind you. You may not become Mozart, but if you just touch one, they may touch millions.

If God sows a seed, God will make it grow. If He implants the desire, He will provide the talent. If God plants a vision, He will make provision.

WISDOM CROSSOVER

Wisdom comes not overnight, an African proverb says.

Wisdom is gained in a slow process of acquiring knowledge, learning from missteps, and plain walking through life.

I make a point of gleaning a morsel of wisdom from every encounter—be it a new friend, a phrase, or a simple gesture. There is plenty of it going around.

The greatest wisdom comes from applying lessons learned in one area to another unlike it.

At home, put to work what you learned in school. Use work skills to improve your play. Take parenting insights to your place of business.

The more unlikely the combination, the more fruitful the synthesis.

What could Economic Theory have in common with parenting a toddler? Can a toddler really teach you how to be a better manager at work?

Children's unencumbered minds are the most delightful sources of wisdom.

Around the time my daughter was five, an ill-fated chain of events forced us to sell our house and live in an awful apartment for a year.

That year would have been far more intolerable had my daughter not called it "the partyment" for all the fun we had in it.

THE TULIP POPLAR

Last summer a rare tornado passed through our region. The powerful winds knocked down trees and destroyed property. Being highly unusual, the storm got the full attention of the local media.

A reporter went to a home leveled by a fallen tulip poplar. "That should surprise no one," his article stated. "Tulip poplars are nothing but big weeds."

That statement aroused in me every prejudice and injustice; recent ones and those from the distant past. How dare he?

Why is the tulip poplar more of a weed than any other tree? Besides, what is wrong with weeds? Aren't they also God's Creation?

Weeds *and* tulip poplars have adapted in their own way to their niche in the world of all living things. Tulip poplars add to the well-being of their ecosystem by providing shade, pollen, and nuts.

They have earned the right to their existence by adapting to their ever-changing environment. The poplar achieved it by profuse regeneration and brisk growth. Others resorted to extensive roots, evergreen needle-like leaves, or extreme economy of water.

In some way, all species have paid a price for their adaptations. Those changes came from necessity for survival, not from the desire to please man.

If anyone is to blame, it was man and his house that came to the poplar and not the other way around.

REACHING HIGHER

As you may know, I am a member of Toastmasters—a club focused on public speaking and leadership skills. I have been also using that forum, fairly but assertively, to promote Quaker know-how.

A number of club members are marketing professionals. They routinely attend gatherings where the latest sales and marketing gimmicks are taught by the best leaders in the field.

I do enjoy the free version of these prohibitively expensive events, provided they are presented in good taste.

Our last program was a recap of a workshop called "Reaching Higher," where the participants were asked to envision ways to spend eighty thousand dollars each and every month.

Winners were cheered, losers chastised. The reason for their loss, they were told, was that they had not dreamed high enough. I don't know anyone who has those kind of dreams. Had I had one, it would have sure been a nightmare.

Toastmasters is democratic. We all get equal time at the pulpit. Needless to say, my next speech will be titled "Reaching Higher."

It will be a different kind of reach—one anchored in Quaker values. I will be reaching higher in spiritual aspirations, not in mammon.

Friends have not had their last laugh yet...

IN AWE

A beech tree can live four hundred years. I have one in my yard. In fact, I have a whole bunch of them, shiny, slender, and seemingly invincible; frozen in time. I have not seen them change in a decade.

But this particular one is unique. Its trunk exceeds many times the others, the canopy is lost somewhere in the sky, and the branches reach out far and wide in all directions. It may be the mother of the patch.

I often sit in its shade pondering the events this tree has lived through. It may have witnessed ten or fifteen generations of humans. It must weigh as much as the number of people equal to its age.

Sitting there, I feel small and insignificant. I am in the shadow of a giant.

For hundreds of years, this tree knew exactly what to do. It knew when to bud, when to bloom and when to shed. It knew which way to grow its roots and its branches. It has stood its ground claiming its spot under the sun. It knew how to fight off its enemies without weapons known to man.

Somehow, all that knowledge has been encrypted in cellulose. I was in awe.

I was even more in awe looking at the tiny four-lobed pod with its miniature nuts.

How could that tiny seed give birth to a centuries-old giant? How could all the knowledge of that giant reside in such a tiny seed?

A TRIP TO WHERE?

After college, I decided to take a low-budget trip with a long-time friend.

I knew where I was going. My friend and I made detailed plans. I knew how much I could spend and when I would return.

We took a flight to London and a ferry to the continent. Trains took us to Amsterdam, Copenhagen, and Munich. On the last leg of the trip, the Orient Express took me from Vienna to Athens with a stopover in my hometown.

Big Ben and Hyde Park, the Red-Light District, the little mermaid, and the Glockenspiel at Marienplatz were cultural icons that we encountered.

The train ride across the mountains and valleys of Greece may fall in the category of spiritual experience. Going to my native home certainly did. But spiritual journeys are different.

We don't know where we are going. There is no arrival time and there is no return. We don't choose whom we go with or whom we encounter. We don't know what to look for or find along the way. There is a price to pay, but we don't know what it will be. That kind of trip may be scary, but the pay-off is worth it.

A spiritual journey is personal. Some milestones will be the same, but no two people will read them alike. I, for one, came to realize "that of God in everyone" includes me! I am the sum-total of everything that ever happened in the Universe. I carry the memory of every star, atom, and organism that ever existed.

THE ROSE OF JERICHO

The desert has mystical powers
Wind and sand and the unforgiving sun
Its powerful agents

Beyond dancing apparitions, death is just one step away
Only thistles and myths bloom in the dunes

The Rose of Jericho is among them

The Rose of Jericho is just that—a thistle—but
In the desert it is more beautiful than a rose in a garden

It is as short-lived as all else in the desert

As the rains end
It dries into a ghostly silhouette with fist-like pods

It is a swift death after a brief and fragile life

Like a sentinel
It braves fierce storms and murderous heat
For many months to come

At last new bursts of rain arrive again

Seemingly in a post-mortem act
The pods pop open
Seeds scatter onto the welcoming moist soil

The cycle of life goes on

Perhaps the thistle wasn't dead after all!

What is death and when is it final?

THE POWER OF THE DEAD

A young woman goes to the shrink for acute depression.

Her anger from an ancient argument had stopped her from speaking to her father for twenty-five years.

Finally, she did go to talk to him, only to learn that he had passed away the prior week. An unbearable guilt engulfed her.

How could death do what life couldn't in all those years?

Does the permanence of death bring on the urge to leave a clean slate?

Is harmony in death more important than harmony in life?

Death needs not to be a terminal severance. The Mormons have a remarkable point of view in this respect.

They see family continuing beyond death. Family members continue to provide spiritual strength well after their departure.

For this reason, more and more people research and document their ancestry.

The knowledge of the past provides continuity and empowerment. It is a connection to generations of ancestors who paved the way for us to be here and to be who we are.

Reliving their struggles and triumphs not only expands the scope of their lives beyond their physical existence but boosts our own sense of purpose.

SOMETHING ABOUT BOB

Bob was a friend and a colleague. He was also a recent born-again Christian, full of excitement and evangelical zeal. I, on the other hand, was a complete neophyte in matters of that sort. That combination was fertile ground for endless lunch-time discussions.

Talking to Bob was always pleasant. I liked hearing his point of view for it did satisfy my curiosity. And Bob was eager to share his newly found wisdom, perhaps harboring hidden hope that, one day, I might become like him.

It should be no surprise that our most memorable talk was about evolution. Bob, of course, was in the creationist camp. I had no real problem with his perspective because if God didn't create those animals, well, then someone else did. To me, it was one and the same thing!

But how could Noah fit them all in the Ark? The size of the Ark was finite. Its dimensions are well known. The land and air species were in the millions. I asked Bob if Noah had all those animals on the boat, in addition to a forty-day food supply.

Bob, a logical guy, recognized the problem at hand and said no. So, all the animals that we now know, I asked, where have they all come from? To my surprise Bob's answer was that…they have evolved.

That conversation, absurd as it may sound, was certainly amusing. It deserves a smile or if not that, perhaps just a shrug. Any other debate on that topic—no matter how scholarly or sophisticated—deserves the same reaction and nothing more.

SOMETHING ELSE ABOUT BOB

I had never before met a guy like Bob. One day, having exhausted our routine biblical discourse, Bob told me he wanted to sell his ancient Volkswagen Beetle.

He had found a buyer who offered a fair price, but Bob refused to sell it to him because...he didn't like him! For me, the sale of a car had always been a financial transaction with the goal of maximizing the value of the asset.

Giving a pet to the wrong person might have caused me remorse, but a car? Silly as it was, I had to concede. Bob did have a point. What the point was is hard to say, but for first time, I witnessed a different kind of logic.

Over time, I lost track of Bob but have not forgotten him or his lessons.

Events came full circle twenty-five years later when I put my long-time home up for sale. The house had charming features and, over the years, I had collected antiques and ornaments to match the style.

In preparation for the sale, I felt an urge to make the house as appealing as I could, an urge that transcended the potential sale incentive. Somehow that urge had to do with Bob.

A buyer did come along and fell completely in love with the place. Her offer reflected that feeling.

A simple real-estate transaction morphed into karmic joy created for strangers by strangers. Selling my house is among my most joyous memories. Thank you, Bob!

QUAKERISM AND CUBISM

By the mid-nineteenth century, painters of Realism had achieved unsurpassable perfection. The advent of photography, however, introduced an alternative medium for capturing the perfection of reality, forcing artists to seek challenges in new modalities.

The first departure was to abandon perfection proper and capture the impression from the subject instead. Other shifts followed. Artists focused on studies of light, color, and movement, and their mutual interplay.

In the span of a few decades, Realism was reduced to Minimalism. Cubism, more than the others, transcends all the natural elements of a painting and focuses strictly on the essence of the subject.

That intriguing evolution of visual arts was still fresh in my mind when I attended my first Quaker meeting. Meeting houses lack décor. The worship is mostly silent. There are no sermons, ceremonies, or sacraments.

Such a scene may shock one accustomed to ornate churches with stained-glass windows and stone sculptures, wood carvings and bone-shaking organs, not to mention the colorful liturgy and the festively attired clergy.

Even though Quaker reductionism originates from the tradition of simplicity, a certain parallel to evolutionary art exists. Both shed the ancillaries in attempt to capture essence.

Cubists—the essence of the subject

Quakers—the essence of the Divine

SPIRITUAL SEPARATION AND OTHER

Creation may be the most baffling story in the Bible.

In the flux of those cataclysmic events, it is easy to overlook the fact that over half of God's effort in Creation was devoted to separation.

God separated the light from the darkness. And there was evening and morning. It was the end of day one.

God separated the waters under and above the firmament. And there was evening and morning, the second day.

God separated the dry land and the seas. And there was evening and morning. A third day.

God made lights in heavens to separate day and night. And there was evening and morning. Day number four.

On the seventh day, God rested.

The series of separations culminated with setting apart rest from work, the separation of the spiritual realm from its physical counterpart.

With so much separation in the world, more attention is due to separations under our control.

Separation of what is essential and what isn't

Separation of what we can and cannot control

Separation between sacred and profane

Above all, time separation for the pursuit of spiritual life

SEPARATION OR SEVERANCE

Uncle Ernie was my favorite uncle. I had great respect for him, for his unshakable equanimity of heart and his stoic philosophy of life. He had been at peace with his troubled life more than anyone I knew.

He was also among my many "victims," whom I kept quizzing about our family history.

At one point, Uncle Ernie told me I should no longer concern myself with certain ancestors whom I had kept asking about.

While reluctant to heed his advice outright, I did consider his view and began to value the benefits of severance.

Assisted by our new information technology, I have managed to reconnect with a handful of old friends, with whom I had lost contact over the years.

I had regretted those separations since we had been close friends, and I felt a void as a consequence.

While we were all glad to have found each other again, I sadly realized that very little was left of our friendships of youth.

After a time, the connections receded again, and this time, most likely for good.

Uncle Ernie's advice came in handy.

I am now able to look at those separations as intentional severance, without regrets or sadness.

A TALE FROM THE ORIENT

Once, there lived an exceedingly rich man. He was surrounded by servants and harems. For decades, his most trusted servant had seen to all his needs. Then one day, the rich man embarked on a journey and left his affairs in his servant's hands.

Upon his return, however, the servant was gone, and so was the pot of gold the rich man had left in the open. The servant was found and arrested. While his guilt was punishable by death, at the trial, the rich man declared the servant innocent.

"The guilt is mine," he said, "for I had tempted my servant beyond his ability to resist it."

I love that tale!

Once upon a time, ages ago, I made a grave error at a new job. I regretted the damage, but more so, I regretted being complicit in the ensuing cover-up. I was torn between gratitude to my boss for saving my job and guilt for playing along.

The tale of the rich man showed me that the fault wasn't all mine. The boss was responsible for my training and for preventing mistakes. In fact, the cover-up was more in his self-interest than mine. The lesson is well known: It takes two to tango.

To a degree, we are bosses. We have a range of duties—at home and in society. We are liable not only for our action but for the lack thereof. We cannot just live a law-abiding life and let others break the law. One should never tolerate nor ignore agents of violence and destruction.

OF GENESIS AND MAN

Consider how the world was made.

On day one, God created heaven and earth. On the second day, He made the firmament and separated it from the waters.

Then God gathered the waters and created dry earth and seas. He filled the earth with seed-yielding plants and fruit-bearing trees. It was day three.

On the fourth day, He made the sun, the moon, and the stars, and on the fifth day filled the waters with fish and the air with flying creatures. Creeping things, beasts of the earth, and cattle followed on the sixth day.

By the end of the sixth day, there was still no sign of man.

Then, at last, God said, "Let us make man in our image!"

God toiled on the heavenly infrastructure for three days, and another three on the living creatures. After all that, the making of man was a snap—an afterthought.

Genesis presents the mind-boggling complexity of God's work in the simplest terms. It took three days of the six to make the earth, and three more days to make everything else. Man came five minutes before midnight.

In spite of it, man sees himself as the center of the world.

A closer look at the math ought to kick in a modicum of humility. It might just raise our holistic view of the Universe around us by one tiny fraction of a notch...

WHO IS GOD?

The year I was born, a restless artist painted a six-foot canvas. It featured a brown background and a vertical red line in its center.

What could that be?

It was a piece of canvas covered with oil paint. That much is fact.

Beyond that, to a trucker, it could be a highway, a curtain to a decorator, or to the artist—the ultimate self-portrait.

In fact, everyone who had ever seen it may have figured something different. Many only see the canvas and the paint.

This canvas is not unlike God.

People give God a variety of attributes as well. Some fear Him, others love Him. Some pray to a benefactor or a guardian, and others yet ignore Him.

Do we know *anything* about God?

If you are reading this text, you are alive and you are here.

Most people will acknowledge that *they* didn't create either themselves or the Universe. And no one could guarantee to be alive tomorrow or the day after.

Can it be said then that there is a force outside of us and beyond our control that is the causation of the Universe?

What should we name it?

ONEMENT

Onement is the name of a brown canvas with a vertical red line. The painting, valued at close to one hundred million dollars, is on display at the Metropolitan Museum of Art in New York City. Thousands of people, every year, try to guess its significance.

Onement stands for being eager and enthused, being healed and restored, for being at peace.

Oddly, onement also stands for being disenchanted, passive, and resigned.

Onement is a state of being reconciled, which is the result of either harmony or alienation.

Onement is a statement about man's condition vis-à-vis the Universe.

Man may be in unison with it and in fellowship with God or apart.

Man cannot grasp void or eternity and is powerless in the face of infinity.

Awed by the encounter, man may retreat to the comforts of avoidance and agnosticism.

A harmonious onement affirms man's existence as the end-product of all that ever existed in the Universe.

Being in that kind of onement is not merely being with God but being part of God and all His perfections.

That is a special onement—a won-ment.

GOD'S PLAN

In the beginning there was tohu and bohu—chaos

That is what Genesis says

Of that chaos, God made a perfect Creation

One may think that creation of that scale
must be the result of a plan

But chaos *can* lead to order

Pebbles thrown into the lake create perfect ripples

Perfect snowflakes form for no apparent reason

Amazing ice crystals grow before the eyes

They are all the result of energy generated without a plan

So a no-plan *is* a plan?

Is there no such thing as a no-plan?

The lack of a plan doesn't make less of Creation

Creation of such complexity *without* a plan
only adds tribute to its Creator

The message seems obvious

Even with random forces at work
All things work out in the end

That is a promising thought

KARMA AROUND US

Karma is said to be the sum total of one's conduct in this life. It dictates one's destiny in the next.

While that may or may not be true, cause and effect occur in this life every day. Simply put, what goes around comes around.

Karma is a collective trust fund. Good and bad go in and out, all the time.

Neighborhoods have one. Neighbors with a high fund balance leave their doors unlocked and their bicycles in the driveway.

Towns have one. In a town of good karma, you can pump gas before paying, leave your car unlocked at the store, and guards will not stand by the door to check your bags when you leave.

Karma is seen every day. Good karma shows in the respect for the law. It is seen in the civility of the people. It is reflected in ordinary commerce, friendly service in restaurants, and by strangers holding the door for the next one who comes or goes.

Countries have karma. A visit to another country makes the business of karma all very clear.

The point of the karma is simple

When the tide is in, everyone's boat rises

We grow good karma together
We are all beneficiaries of the trust fund

OF MUSTARD SEEDS AND MINISTRY

The Kingdom of Heaven is like the mustard seed, says Matthew of the Gospels. It is the tiniest of all seeds, but it grows to the largest tree in the garden.

Birds of the air come to perch on its branches. They build nests creating something new and totally unimagined. Indirectly, the tiny mustard seed creates a new, wonderful reality.

The same goes to Quaker worship. As the mustard seed sprouts in fertile soil, here, each message puts a new reality into motion, for once spoken, the reach of the words is unfathomable. No one can tell who will be touched. No one can tell when and how.

Meeting for worship is a balance of spirit-led messages and silence. Some Friends prefer an abundance of silence. Others look forward to the message of the Spirit, for a lost message is a lost chance. If you don't ask, the answer is always no.

No Friend should come to worship determined to share a message or with a mind made up not to. There are Friends, however, who are wary of excessive caution in worship. Marie was right to question the hesitation.

Invariably, even in old age and frail physique, Marie, whose voice was barely audible, had words of wisdom to share in worship. "Why aren't Friends speaking," she once voiced her frustration. "They must be thinking something!"

Marie has been long gone, but her admonition is still here, fresh in my mind.

BETWEEN WORSHIP AND MEDITAION

Some cultures view worship as veneration. That view had been one reason for my struggle understanding worship. Others say that worship is going to church, which I find even more confusing; going to church to worship is going to church to worship...

While veneration is of something, Friends do not worship something; they simply worship. Friends worship comes with a qualifier—silent expectation. The silent part seemed pretty clear. Aha! So Friends worship is meditation! Group meditation was something I always wanted to do.

The worship part clicked too eventually. Worship derives from worth-ship—a deed of worth, a worthwhile act. In fact, for Friends, worship is the most important thing they do. And collective worship creates a sacred place, a place unmatched elsewhere.

I couldn't figure out, though, why I had trouble meditating in worship. Centering down and clearing one's heart and mind are the very things you do in meditation. It may be the expectation part that sets worship and meditation apart.

Meditation removes the senses from reality into the world within body and mind. In expectant worship, the world does disappear; body and mind are put on hold, but the heart opens up to a universe of a different dimension.

It is a spiritual dimension, for expectant worship is meditation in the presence of the Divine. That is a connection to a limitless spiritual online—the ultimate internet. Who can possibly meditate with that?

CONTINUING QUERIES

How does truth prosper among us?

Are we mindful of the divine presence?

How do we honor the Light of God in others?

How do we share our spiritual life with Friends?

What have we done to enhance our spiritual lives?

What have we done to enhance others' spiritual lives?

What have we done to spread Friends spiritual message?

Do we readily ask for clearness?

Are our thoughts aligned with the Spirit?

What have we done to prepare for worship?

Are we in the spirit of meeting in our daily lives?

Are our actions aligned with Friends testimonies?

Have we provided spiritual space to our loved ones?

What have we done to share our witness in the world?

How do we apply our worshipful presence in meeting?

Are you proactively enjoying your life?

How do we shine our Light in the world?

OVERCOME EVIL WITH GOOD

People alone are responsible for what happens inside their heads. That is popular wisdom.

I, for one, have failed to stamp out old demons, large and small. They pop into my mind uninvited and constantly beg for replays.

"So, okay already! I could have done better," I say. "Now let's move on!" There have been no takers.

Then I received a gift. "Overcome evil with good." It worked even before trying.

Good and evil are not only antonyms but antidotes. Antidotes are specific. A snake bite is not treated with aloe but with a precise mix that neutralizes the venom.

Abstract notions only register in a particular form, for the same reason. Some explanations may do the job for certain people but frustrate others.

So, to counter failure-hungry demons, or for simple enjoyment, recall the satisfaction from that which *had been* done right!

There is much of that and much more yet to come

Counter demons with future solutions

Plan to apply lessons of the past

Set eyes on do-overs

Do good for its own sake

MINISTRY AND SHOPPING BAGS

What is between ministry and shopping bags?

I shall start off with ministry, as it is my favorite topic to talk about. I believe everyone has the ability and the desire to minister. Ministries are large and small.

We often focus on a community vigil or a rally in Washington D.C., but the small actions are what really count. Drops of water carry mountains to the sea. Grains of sand have carved nature's largest monuments.

Now to shopping bags.

When it comes to shopping bags, it has been paper or plastic. But I bought two canvas ones from the store I go to—the first store in town to offer them.

I think of all the people I pass in the parking lot on Sunday afternoons who see me walking around with them, empty or full; hundreds, perhaps thousands of people.

The message to them is not that some guy likes to walk around the parking lot with shopping bags. The message is that there is yet another person who is concerned enough about the environment to go through the trouble.

At first, I only used those bags where I had bought them. I then realized there was even a stronger message in carrying them everywhere, especially to stores that didn't offer their own. Here comes a shopping-bag crusader!

*Since the first writing, every store in town began offering canvas bags of their own. Lone crusader no more.

JANE

Jane, a long-time member of our meeting, passed away this week after a prolonged illness.

A memorial service was held the day before yesterday in this room to celebrate Jane's life and to mourn her passing.

The room overflowed with family and friends.

Dozens of people spoke with love and admiration about Jane and about the impact she had had on their lives.

I can still feel their energy and vibrations today.

The endless ways in which we can touch other lives never ceases to amaze me.

I want to paraphrase one message. It was not only the funniest but also encapsulates my feelings toward the departed.

The message was offered by an older gentleman, Jane's longtime acquaintance and friend.

He had been especially touched in his life by Jane's actions and had the highest regards for her—both in life and in her passing.

"Jane is not gone," he said. "She is still here with us.

She just moved to the place where she needs to be.

In fact, after this service, I am going to ask her to look for a good apartment for me."

FROM REASON TO PURPOSE

Forest Gump is in Vietnam. His platoon has been ambushed, and Bubba—his best friend—has been shot and is dying. With his last words, Bubba asks Forrest: "Why Forrest, why?" To this Forrest answers: "You've been shot, Bubba!"

It was a correct answer, but what Bubba was really asking: Why me? Why does Bubba, who has never hurt anyone, deserve this?

The "Book" holds that the righteous will be rewarded and the wicked be punished. Then it tells the story of Job, the most righteous of men, afflicted by every earthly ill.

The Book offers a rationale: The sins of fathers affect three and four generations. That may be so in the big picture as our descendants will carry the burdens of our economic, political, and ecological legacy.

But I cannot imagine what awful deeds our forefathers could have committed to explain the tragedies in this world—earthquakes, hurricanes, disease.

"Mysterious are the ways of the Lord," the Book continues. While that may invite resignation, I find it redemptive. Mystery suggests a need for a broader view. Instead of asking why, we should perhaps ask what for.

Tragedies teach valuable lessons. But a broader view may point to the fact that our lives have been out of balance with the world that we have put ourselves in harm's way.

"There is reason for everything" may thus become "there is a purpose to everything."

HOW TRUE IS TRUTH

God transcends human comprehension.

That may explain why I, as many others, struggle with big-picture concepts like religion and spirituality.

Meeting is the place for sorting them out, and meeting enables each and every one to find their individual path to discovery and revelation.

I not only learn a kernel of truth every day, but I am becoming increasingly convinced that the answers are simple rather than complex.

"Truth is the word of God" implies that the ultimate truth stands regardless of creeds, which Bible version we read, and regardless whether Jesus was the Son of God or not.

*   *

Friends testimonies set a high bar. Peace, justice, and truth call for absolutes. But there are no absolutes in life. There is no perfect justice, total peace, or absolute truth, and there will never be.

All Friends can do is to aspire to them. Living our testimonies means daily discernment. How do we best approximate our ideals? What priorities do we set? Where do we compromise?

We may not know what the exact truth is and may never find out.

By claiming that truth is the word of God, however, we recognize its utmost importance.

KNOWLEDGE, WISDOM, SPIRITUALITY

A magnet on my fridge says: There is no knowledge without wisdom.

I can relate to that. A friend comes to mind who can recite baseball stats from the thirties and the shoe sizes of the entire NBA.

I have never thought such fact hoarding was knowledge, and frankly, his "dissertations" became increasingly annoying.

The magnet goes on to say: There is no wisdom without spirituality.

At first, that sounded like another clever catchphrase. But then, the dictionary came to the rescue.

The dictionary says wisdom is the knowing of what is true and what is right, and if I may add to that, also what is relevant.

Fortunately, the dictionary further elaborates to say that wisdom also implies sound judgment, discernment, and insight.

While sound judgment is gained through education and life experience, discernment and insight are products of spiritual practice.

With that awareness, I venture to say that my magnet has a point!

There is no knowledge without wisdom, and there is no wisdom without spirituality.

FAIRYTALE WISDOM

The beautiful fairytale princess falls under a spell and sleeps one hundred years. At last, she is awakened by a handsome young prince. They fall in love and live happily ever after.

But what if the fairytale is merely an allegory?

What if the princess wasn't really sleeping all that time, only devoid of passion and purpose? What if she spent her life without feelings and emotion, as many others do?

Many of the enigmatic stories of the Bible sound like fairytales. But what if the opaque biblical words, like our loved fairytales, hide messages of vital importance?

Could those tales have been purposefully created in a language easy to understand in their time?

Genesis is full of such tales, and the story of Eden leads the pack. But what seems like one more absurd fairytale may have profound implications today.

The sight of an oversize orange moon on the horizon is an astonishing scene, but Earth rise on the moon must be overwhelming.

The enormous blue-and-white ball engulfing the lunar sky is awe-inspiring even in photographs. One must wonder at the miracle of our exquisite planet.

Aren't *we* living in Paradise today? The Earth is good and forgiving. We, however, seem to have lost sight of the biblical moral. At the going rate, we may lose the real Eden.

POWER OF THE EXAMPLE

One good thing about politics is the birth and rise of slogans. The Obama presidential campaign gave birth to "Leadership by the power of example and not by the example of power."

To me it was a winner as soon as it first aired. Slogans are portable to many conditions.

"The Power of Example" was exactly what *I* had in mind to caption the power of personal witness.

To carry out the ministry of a spirit-led life you only need to *be*. Being you will have great impact on friends and strangers alike.

There is a tendency to assert power, if for no other reason, because the privilege of rank is convenient.

The dynamic of power is clear cut, and the use of power yields immediate results. In the short term, the example of power is effective.

Nowhere is that more evident than in a parent-child interaction. It is much easier to say do so because I said so, than do so because *I* did so.

It takes a leap of faith to choose a path with no visible results. It is a leap of faith to trust unseen forces to take root, or a steady trickle to swell into the current that will touch the many.

Slogans flesh out ideas. They can be powerful catalysts. The Power of Example is one—even if born in the heat of rhetoric.

ALL THESE FRIENDS

On the first Sunday of the fall season, the meeting house was packed. It was refreshing to see everyone after the long and lazy summer that scatters people in all different directions. I felt great welcoming energy.

A Friend spoke and casually noted how nice it was to see so many people gathered as Friends. That casual comment was anything but casual to me. "People gathered as Friends" has been on my mind ever since.

On the surface, there is no distinction between a random crowd sitting in a room and a group of gathered Friends. Quaker worship can be many things to many people; to strangers, it is almost inexplicable.

Even I wondered at times.

In the doldrums of summer was meeting in gathered silence or just passively estivating?

But the fact remained. On that Sunday morning, all those people chose to come to meeting!

The weather was most pleasant. They could have done a number of other things. Some had traveled great distances to attend, others made special arrangements to free up their time.

For their own personal reasons, they chose to come to meeting instead. They chose to gather as Friends!

It was their most important thing to do

It was *my* best and the most meaningful meeting

A ROADSIDE AZALEA

Even though this story is part of the fallout of the currently waged presidential campaign, it is as much about gardening as about politics.

On the roadside down the street, there is an azalea bush unlike any other. Its color resembles more the pale magenta of a neon billboard than any floral palette.

Following the spring bloom, I "adopted" a snippet which prospered in its new home.

But with the approach of fall and political tempers on the rise, I was dismayed to see that next to my cherished azalea there was a campaign poster of the *wrong* party.

In the heat of the battle, I vowed that if the "wrong" party wins the election, I would get rid of my transplant.

The truth is, I really didn't want to do that. The plant was doing quite well, and I had been obsessed with its color.

Political passions, valid as they may be, can have far-reaching implications. On second thought, I came to realize that my reaction was absurd.

On second thought, the election wasn't really about the right or wrong party. Politics aside, at the end of the day, we all want the same thing.

We want to maintain the fabric of our communities and to live amicably with our neighbors.

Weren't those the goals of the election?
Wasn't that exactly what we were fighting for?

ALL OR NOTHING

A school principal's testimony

A sudden death of a young parent is a devastating tragedy to the family, and to our small school community it was a complete shock.

As principal, I wanted to do *something* to help, but there wasn't anything I could do to change what had happened.

Often, people are stymied by the chasm between what they want to do and what they can do. Because of it, frequently, they are frozen into inaction.

Do all or do nothing! Since I can't change the situation, I won't do anything.

But reality is not black or white. Even if I cannot change the tragic event, by carrying out my ordinary functions and offering support, I still serve as a block of the world that had previously been intact.

We are not expected to do miracles or to fix every problem around us. But we can all help greatly just by being ourselves.

In a time of loss, what is left intact is what we still have. Being part of that consistency is in itself of great help.

And the knowledge of being helpful is very comforting.

I AM HAPPY

An elderly gentleman reports to his retirement home.

On the way to the elevator, the nurse describes to him his new room. She is surprised by the man's excitement.

"You haven't even seen your room," she says.

"You are right," the man quips, "but I already like it. I had decided I liked it before I came!"

Happiness is a decision. While intellectually, one can decide to be happy regardless of circumstances, putting it into action it is not so easy.

Recently, we heard the author of *Amish Grace*.

He spoke about the ways the Amish managed to overcome the horrible school murder in their community and forgive the perpetrator.

What helped them was practice. The Amish practice forgiveness as a routine of their religious life. Can happiness or the decision to become happy be practiced?

The short answer of course is yes. A spiritual life does facilitate the pursuit of personal goals.

Could the Amish have achieved forgiveness as individuals? It may be a hypothetical, perhaps pointless question. Of greater merit is to ask how we can create a collective practice that leads to a state of happiness. After all, a community is greater than the sum total of its individual members.

A LESSON FROM ELLIS

In his ninety-six years of life, Ellis touched many people in meeting and in the community. Family, friends and public officials attested to that by sharing loving memories, contributions, and quite appropriately for an old-time farmer—chicken jokes.

Ellis was a pillar of constancy. Although he never spoke in worship, he had never missed one, had never changed his seat, or…fallen asleep. Through his unwavering actions, Ellis embodied the essence of meeting for worship.

I had often wondered what lay behind those big blue eyes and stern face. It wasn't easy getting to know Ellis. Once we made special arrangements to have him over for dinner, but a mid-March snowstorm decided otherwise.

Finally, I cornered him one day at another dinner event and asked him point blank: "Ellis, what do you think about in meeting for worship?" "Good things—I hope," was his response.

"That isn't how I do things" is peculiar to Friends way of speaking. Although I have never heard Ellis say that, it was precisely what defined him: a man who lived by uncompromising principles.

It is good to be in the world of such a man, even temporarily. The memory of Ellis's statue-like presence on the facing bench will be a permanent reminder that principles can triumph over expediency.

Judging from all the love showered on Ellis, one thing became crystal clear. You can lead a fruitful life without compromising close-to-the-heart principles.

SINGLE BLACK FEMALE

"Single black female seeks companionship. I am a very good girl who loves to play. I enjoy long walks in the woods, riding in your truck, hunting, fishing, and cozy winter nights by the fire.

Candlelight dinners will have me eating out of your hand. I'll be at your front door when you come home from work, wearing only what nature has given me.

Call 414 809-8585, and ask for Daisy."

Fifteen thousand men answered this ad, and found themselves talking to the Atlanta SPCA about an eight-month-old Labrador.

This wouldn't warrant mention if it weren't for a fellow named Seriously Black who was not only featured recently in the *Friends Journal** but also happens to be a personal acquaintance of one of our distinguished Friends in meeting.

Seriously Black is the friendliest of fellows. He walks cheerfully over the Earth answering that of God in others, just as George Fox had prescribed.

His enthusiasm is innate and universal, notwithstanding race, gender, or age. To Seriously Black, all men are created equal.

It is unlikely that Seriously Black has gathered his convictions from George Fox. In fact, the exact opposite may be true. See, Seriously Black is a miniature, curly, black, four-legged poodle!

* Friends Journal is a national Quaker Monthly

HONORING REAT

Reat exuded gentleness, empathy, and love. She had been adamant about one thing, though. Reat wanted her reluctant husband to wear a necktie to her memorial service. He could no longer be present, but Reat's wish was met in abundance. The family—men, women, and kids, the entire facing bench—came in wearing good-humored neckties.

Sharing by family, friends, and Friends flowed well beyond the slated hour-long memorial service. One Friend capped off an emotional message lamenting: "And now, Reat is gone." I was taken aback by the remark. With all the living memories we had heard, I felt Reat's presence very much with us in the room.

But the momentous question lingered. Was Reat gone or was she still here?

*   *

Throughout her life, Reat blessed those around her with many gifts and in many ways. Those gifts were free to all. She had bestowed them unconditionally, without strings attached.

Granted, no one takes those gifts lightly, but in time, new matters and concerns surface, memories fade and become forgotten. Reat *will* be gone. What if, though, we assume those gifts were given to us as endowment?

A spiritual endowment, as any other endowment, comes with a fiduciary onus. With that, the burden is on all those who benefited from Reat's gifts to put them to work wisely. To honor Reat, we must in our own deeds and actions be the conduit for her everlasting Light.

A FRIGID VISITATION

It was a blustery Saturday morning when I chauffeured my folks to the train station. No wonder it felt good to sit in the sun-lit cozy car and shake off the platform chill.

Adrift from the curious early-morning adventure, I just sat there in the parking lot torn by the harsh choice of going to the supermarket or a quick retreat to bed.

The row of lonesome houses across from the lot had always intrigued me. Now, a group of people milling around the porches grabbed my attention. I conjured an early house party or a family breakfast get-together.

As I idly pondered the outside world, a gentleman left the crowd and approached my car. The *Watchtower* was peeking from his coat. Aha, Jehovah Witnesses!

I rolled down my window, and said as I always do on such occasion: "Hi, I am a Quaker from Downingtown Meeting, and I'll be happy to weigh any spiritual matters with you." After chatting for a while, I reluctantly accepted a copy of his pamphlet. It said this:

"Having solved the question of how to make a living and having surrounded ourselves with once unthinkable luxuries, we are left to wonder why we live and what is the meaning and the purpose of life.

Ignoring the question is like ignoring a pebble in your shoe."

The answers that followed did not speak to my condition, but my frigid early-bird doldrums were clearly over. It may have been a quick visit from God...

TOUCHED BY THE LONE RANGER

With yet another obscure clue in the weekend crossword puzzle, it was time to catch up with The Lone Ranger.

I soon learned that there was a film with all the answers.

It covered the radio history of the show, described the logic behind the characters, and contained the very first episode aired on television in the fifties.

The amateurism of the show was amusing. The feature reminded me of a show called *Save the Black Ferret* that my fifth-grade daughter had taped on a camcorder.

The props seemed home-made, the dialog elementary, and the mask...hmm...Did the Lone Ranger expect anyone not to recognize him?

But the Lone Ranger had principles!

> To have a friend, man must be one
> Be ready to fight for what is right
> Make the most of what you have
> God made firewood, man just needs to gather it
> Man must pay the world for all he has taken
> We all have the power to make the world better

An obscure crossword clue has led me to spirituality. I shouldn't have been surprised. It is all around us!

The Lone Ranger would say: "God put spirituality there, man must just gather it."

The creed of the Lone Ranger is no different. God had created it. Man only needs to find it.

FACEBOOK MINISTRY

I joined Facebook to be with the in-crowd. Okay, and to be cool. In the eyes of my teen-age daughter, my stock skyrocketed overnight. "Wow, my dad is really smart!"

I have only taken baby steps in it because there is so much to learn. The place is replete with walls and gifts, poking, and even a cat book.

I had had the same challenge as I first attended a Quaker meeting. Queries and advises, clearness and eldering... Excuse me, what did you say?

Like meeting, Facebook is a community. Ironically, its members are also called friends.

Friends, there and here, seek fellowship. Here we gather for weekly worship. There, it is a virtual but perpetual version thereof. Here we share thoughts by messages— there by posts.

I have been more at ease writing on someone else's wall as a direct response to their post than posting on my own.

What was about me that could be newsworthy enough? Why would anyone care about my particular condition?

Then a parallel occurred: ministry by personal witness.

Whether reflected in vocal ministry or in daily deeds, we carry out our actions because, in our view, they are worthy. We attribute to them a certain degree of merit.

Who will be touched by them, how, and when, remains a mystery.

WHERE PEACE IS FOUND

Friends Hymnal is a treasure trove of music and verse. The tunes we sing on Sundays often ring in my ears for weeks to come.

Teach Me to Stop and Listen may be the simplest yet the most captivating one of all. The lean but profound lyrics capture the essence of the entire Quaker experience.

Teach me to stop and listen
Teach me to center down
Teach me the use of silence
Teach me where peace is found

Teach me to hear your calling
Teach me to search your word
Teach me to hear in silence
Things I have never heard

Then when it's time for moving
Grant it that I may bring
To every day and moment
Peace from a silent spring

Find in silence peace for your soul
Take time-out for its sake
Take time-out to hear another voice

Search for the word of the Divine
Find your calling
Find new revelation again and again

Meeting is a silent spring of peace
That power doesn't stop at the door
Bring it to every day and moment
Bring it to your calling
Bring it to your life

TO BE THANKFUL

It is Thanksgiving—a time to ponder our blessings

I am thankful for my family
For having each other and
For having a spiritual life together

I am thankful for my spiritual home
For my spiritual community

Above all
I am thankful for the gift of life
Each day's gift of life

Blessed art thou who giveth life
Who has sustained us and
Has brought us to this day

This blessing is on a rock in my garden
I see it from my window
A daily reminder of that day's gift of life

I affirm this gift to myself

What will I do with this day of life?
The question energizes me

As steward of a sacred gift
I feel at liberty to accept or reject
Intrusions on this precious treasure

I take stock at day's end
Am I fulfilled by my choices?

A HEROINE NAMED JOAN

Alberto Baez left his home in Mexico to shepherd a Latino congregation in Brooklyn. His son, Albert, meant to follow him in ministry but ultimately yielded to his love for science.

As a nuclear physicist in WWII, Albert refused to work on the Manhattan project and spurned lucrative Defense-sector careers.

Those willing to make such sacrifice on moral grounds may be dismayed when others take their place. "If I don't do this someone else will," one might say.

Then Joan "happened." Joan's first act of civil disobedience was as a teenager, when she refused to take part in an air-raid drill. Civil-rights marches and resistance to the war in Vietnam, the fight for international human rights, and the fight against poverty seemed all natural to follow.

Throughout her life, Joan has shown unparalleled courage. Her willingness to sacrifice exceeded that of her father. Joan has created a musical legacy of international renown that has fueled the ideals and has galvanized the actions of a whole generation.

By any measure, Joan Baez is an extraordinary human being and Friend. Did Joan occur by happenstance? Most likely not! Joan's father was supplanted by another physicist, but his sacrifice and witness—as often the case— had unforeseen and far reaching effect.

Albert may have only touched one person, but Joan has touched millions.

THE 100 GREATEST WARS

In a wonderful little book, a history professor from Massachusetts has captured the one hundred most important wars of the human race; the top one hundred wars.

All kinds of wars are in there. There is the cold war, the civil war, and the Zulu war. There is the war of Roses and Jenkins's-ear war. There is a seven-year and a thirty-year, an eighty-year, and a one hundred-year war.

For twenty-five hundred years, brave men rode horses and camels, chariots, and tanks. They sailed ships and flew planes. Many millions perished. Untold fortunes were spent to destroy even greater fortunes.

Each war in the book is told and illustrated on one page. There is no room for glorification. There are facts only— one hundred pages of gruesome facts.

These are the stories of the greatest leaders of mankind. Some wear helmets, others turbans, while others yet don crowns or wigs. Some are clad in armor, others in golden mantles. They all excelled in their affairs and were impelled by irresistible, and at times, divinely inspired motives.

Nonetheless, by the end of all that greatness and the bravura of one hundred stories, it is hard to remember why one king was right while the other wrong, or what exactly did they try to accomplish.

Over millennia, because of this greatness and in tandem with it, mankind has borne an exorbitant, if imaginable sacrifice. Is the world better today as a result?

A FARMER IN MAINE

On a late-spring day, a Maine farmer was working his field. Once again, the rocks have "grown in" over the winter.

The farmer was plucking them out and heaping them into a narrow wall along the country road. Some New York visitors touring the area came by to examine the strange wall.

"Excuse me sir," said one "May I ask you why you are building a wall twice as high as wide?"

Annoyed by the tourists roaming around his fields, the farmer felt in the mood for a chuckle:

"I always build walls twice higher than wide so when the storm blows them over they will be twice wider than high."

The Maine Farmer was Francis Brown's favorite anecdote.

Were the New-Yorkers amused by the wry humor? We don't know, but walls sure aren't built for fair weather.

Structures are designed for the harshest conditions. An ideal wall would be one that gets stronger with each storm.

Are our lives built on solid rock and wide foundations, or are they vulnerable to the effects of storms?

Our protective walls should not lie in ruins even if knocked down by indomitable forces but grow twice stronger.

Life on the edge can only go on under an optimal state of affairs. To endure, it needs fundamental change in the design of its foundation.

AN ARMY OF SOULS

At one phase of my military service, I was posted in a bustling base with loads of equipment and thousands of personnel.

There were hundreds of paratroopers and pilots, drivers and mechanics, cooks and officers, clerks and technicians, gunners and guards. They all went about their assigned tasks. Some wore fatigues, others crew suits or greasy work clothes.

There were hierarchies based on chains of command and chains of command based on the seniority of rank.

Once a week, however, a festive dinner was held at the base. On that occasion, all personnel wore their standard blue and grey street uniforms. Gone were the mechanics and the cooks. There was no telling between the gunners and the clerks.

No matter what they had done beforehand, on that night, they were all reduced to their common denominator: the blues and greys they had on. On that night, for a brief moment, it felt as if we were all together as one.

*   *

We don't wear uniforms in meeting, but for a short hour and a common purpose, we do leave our former identities behind. By shedding our worldly layers, we are left to rejoice in the dignity of being spiritual human beings.

Regardless of the hierarchies of our occupations during the week, in worship, we submit to be vessels for the Spirit. It is a different kind of army: an assembly of souls.

74

FRIENDLY SIN

I have seen the plight of some "sinner" friends who had embraced being "bad" and shouldered great guilt from it.

Even though I have never considered myself "bad," in the aftermath of failures, I, too, felt plenty of guilt.

But being human means stumbling at times. The more we strive for perfection, the more we fail; the higher we reach, the deeper we fall.

And "sin" isn't all black and white. Like all the other clouds it, too, has a silver lining. Take the so called deadly sins.

The sins of omission are sins of not living in the present. Who is entirely innocent of lust and envy; the lust for another place or time, the envy of another's belongings?

Gluttony, greed, and wrath—the "deadly" sins of commission—are likely to succumb to simple temperance.

*   *

Engaging one's gifts in works of the Spirit and joyfulness in God's Creation are the worthiest of all virtues.

Spiritual sloth that prevents them *is* the deadliest of sins but also the easiest to fix with a simple dose of Friendly Light.

And pride, the source of all the others, pride that distorts the view of one's place in God's Creation, is cured by plain Quaker medicine:

There is that of God in everyone

SPIRITUAL SMORGASBORD

The owner of the Chinese restaurant next to my office may have been the man who invented lunch buffets.

The Chinese are known to slave away in their restaurants at all hours, and that may have been something his American wife was reluctant to do.

"Look," she may have told him "We are here day and night; let them pick their own food!"

Lunch buffets spread quickly. In short order, Chinese restaurants and others followed suit. In this town at least, my guy had set the trend.

Substance trumps form, they say. Here too, choice and speed outweighed waitressing courtesies.

Smorgasbord—the mother of all buffets—is a Swedish brainstorm. Smorgasbords lay out all choices in full view. Seeing and smelling are more potent than fancy menus.

Wouldn't it be cool if spirituality were offered in buffet-style smorgasbord?

Spiritual seekers could sample all that is before them instead of reading menus in dark restaurants.

In lieu of wasted full-course meals, they could assemble custom plates of spiritual food fit for their palate.

Each new addition would enrich their spiritual wellspring.

Quakers might just be onto something

A REBBE FOR FRIENDS

The jumbo jet was jam packed except a tempting seat next to mine. The passengers were buckled up for takeoff, but the plane was on hold. A Hasid man had been wrongly seated next to a woman.

Before long, a young Hasid man was sitting in the empty seat by me. He apologized for the inconvenience, but pointed out the need to avoid the unwarranted temptations that may come from sitting next to a woman.

Having not talked to a Hasid before, I was eager to ask some questions. Why was he going to New York? What kind of work did he do? Where did he live? The answers were all the same: The Rebbe.

He was sent to New York by the Rebbe. He worked for the Rebbe and lived near the Rebbe. The Rebbe had arranged his marriage, taught his kids, told him how to vote, and paved his spiritual path.

A Rebbe is a leader and a mentor. Rebbes have loyal followers. Thousands still revere the Lubavitcher Rebbe after his death. The Rebbe lays out the blueprint for all facets of life and makes all key decisions for his flock.

For a moment, I thought, wow, Rebbes were cool. Maybe Quakers could use one. Quakers are the other end of the rainbow. As stewards of their own spirituality, they do chart their own spiritual path, but they must also take charge of every single decision in their lives.

But then, it hit me. How does the Rebbe know all that? He either makes it up or...he listens to the Holy Spirit. Now wait. That's what Quakers do...

GOOBYE CHARLIE, YOU FUNNY GUY...

A funny guy:

"Charlie went to the state hospital to talk to his wife Ginny, who worked there as a nurse. When asked who wants to see her, Charlie said her boyfriend.

Because of the tight security and because the receptionist knew that Jeannie was married, security was called. Rather than getting Ginny, soon, Charlie got a whole lot more instead."

A third-grade friend:

"Charlie and I go back sixty years. We had shared a passion for trucks—first toys, then real ones. We kept the toy ones under the porch at Charlie's house, and we made tracks for them in the back of his yard.

More things followed later, and we parted ways to pursue different things. But we never stopped being friends."

A wholesome life:

"I would be thrilled to have a third-grade friend speak at my memorial service. Charlie is fortunate to have been surrounded by many loving people—family, colleagues, and friends. Charlie lived a wholesome life.

I say this because regardless of how many cars we own, no matter how big our houses are, or what titles we have at our jobs, at the end of the day, only one thing matters.

Charlie had a wholesome life because of the people who had surrounded him throughout his life."

OF CONTINUING REVELATION

Spring is time of magic in the garden. Every day, a new page opens up in full color.

The all-encompassing, spring-heralding yellow of the forsythias starts the show. The navy-blue beds of grape hyacinth and the bright red clusters of tulips follow suit. By mid-May, the tricolor blankets of phlox set the garden on fire.

For the past several years, I have spent countless days in my garden moving rocks and plants, terracing and weeding, and moving more rocks and plants.

Something is always happening out there—spring or not—every day. Plants have feelings. If unhappy, they are quick to let you know. You must accommodate them right away, or else.

Something is new every day. Not only that, but somehow miraculously, I have always seemed to know what to next do in that garden, hour after hour, day after day, year after year. I wondered if continuing revelation had been my guide.

Suddenly, an odd feeling came over me.

What if one day I go out there and see no change? What if, suddenly, I don't know what to do next?

It then occurred to me that continuing revelation is life itself. If revelation were to stop for me one day, I would be either done but more likely dead.

Not dead in body, perhaps, but dead in Spirit.

LESSSONS FROM THE SPIRIT

A "leading" is a conviction or course of action inspired by the Spirit. I had such a leading not long ago. My leading urged me to create and conduct a Quaker orientation class.

In principle, such leading is discerned in meeting channels in order to arrive at what is known as the sense of meeting. The process can be lengthy and laborious. There is no telling what the outcome will be.

A leading of the Spirit entails yielding to discernment by the community and acceptance of its discerned sense.

And there is the rub.

How do I yield to my leading to go ahead and accept the delay and the possible rejection at the same time?

Then, a new leading hit me. The Spirit led me to a favorite quote: "You may be only one person in the world, but you are the world to one person."

I am the world to one person: me.

I followed my new leading. I researched, prepared, and perfected my Quaker class presentation. For me.

I did it, I watched it, and I liked it. I enjoyed my class, and I have fulfilled my leading.

I am prepared to accept the sense of meeting either way.

I am equally excited to lead the class or to let it go—both at the same time.

SIX MONTHS TO LIVE

Jackie was a young woman at my work. One day, when I came back from lunch, Jackie was outside fiddling with a hand-held game.

"Hi Jackie, what are you doing?" I asked in passing. "Oh, nothing just killing time," she replied. One month later Jackie was dead.

There has never been a time or a place with more abundance and longer lives than here and now. Still, at end of life, people often scramble to achieve their life aspirations in the eleventh hour.

The encounter led me to probe my own life aspirations:

Do I live in peace, harmony, and forgiveness?
Are my goals clear and well defined?
Do I make good use of every day's gift of life?
Do I invest enough time and energy in my children?
Do I freely share my God-given gifts with others?
How often do I say: This has been the best day of my life?
What legacy will I leave behind?
Will the world be a better place because I lived?

When my time comes, I wish no regrets, no tears, or sadness. I wish that my children would throw a party and celebrate all the fun we had had together. Maybe I will send the invitations myself—ahead of time.

Friends are stewards of everything. They are stewards of the Earth and all its resources. Why not add one more item to the list?

Our own precious time on Earth

IS THE WORLD GETTING BETTER?

While the peace testimony is at the core of Friends beliefs, mankind, in its entire history, has been steeped in a culture of war. At times, it seems as if "war first" has been man's only modus operandi, the only choice and the only course of action. Thus, Friends may find solace in this story:

By 1700, the British traders had outmaneuvered the French in the lucrative Canadian fur trade. The French had to fight back. With arms, that is. They led a brilliant campaign and wiped out the British trading posts.

Fast-forward a few hundred years. The Exton Mall in Pennsylvania was built in the 1970s in response to the residential sprawl in the county. Sears was the main anchor store and, as the sole department store in the area, had enjoyed twenty years of undisputed monopoly.

Before the new millennium set in, the mall was expanded. Two new department stores were added to where Sears had been king. The new competition was deemed not only undesirable but intolerable.

The renovated complex had barely opened when a ragtag gang trained in the shadows and equipped with powerful explosives arrived at the mall. In the dark of the night, they simply blew up the competing stores and went home.

Hold it! No need to call Homeland Security yet. It is only a hypothetical if absurd scenario. It takes the absurd to refocus what time has erased. In the days of the fur trade, it would have been quite real. It could have been quite real in our time as well had the world not gotten better.

LOVE THY NEIGHBOR

Ask people you know to think of the five most important human beings in their lives. Then ask them, from one to five, what their own position was on the list.

Most listed will be spouses and children, parents and friends. But do not be surprised. No one has even considered putting themselves on it.

People may feel that being on the list, let alone on its top, is simply selfish. Yet, how long can you or anyone else attend to the needs of others without being attended to?

Considering yourself unimportant implies that you expect someone else take care of you. That is far more selfish. To effectively serve others, you must be number one on the list—cared for and loved.

A neglected person becomes resentful, and in time, lousy company. And self is one with whom you must spend most of your time; round-the-clock, in fact. That alone is a good practical reason.

If you must have an ethical excuse, use the Golden Rule. "Love thy neighbor as thyself," it says. The closest neighbor is you.

Love your neighbor as you love yourself is a funny thing. Some people may conclude that if they don't love themselves, it is okay to hate others.

The Golden Rule doesn't imply or condone that, of course.

The Golden Rule takes self-love for granted

LOCUS FOCUS

A pebble thrown into a pond creates expanding ripples in the water. They are the strongest at the point of impact— the locus of the action.

The locus of an earthquake is its epicenter. Physical loci are immovable regardless of how much Californians may wish they went elsewhere.

But matters of the Spirit have no fixed loci. A witness can pick the locus of choice, with far-reaching consequences.

*   *

Vocal ministry is like the pebble thrown into the pond. It reverberates far and wide and when least expected. It first speaks to Friends in meeting who are likely to speak to others. But it may be the speaker who is affected the most.

"That of God in everyone," Friends core belief, sets the locus in others—far from where it counts the most.

The loci of peace, justice, and stewardship is the world. But they have no meaning if they don't apply to me first.

*   *

Choose a locus close to home

Let "everyone" include you

Let your leadings into your own heart

Let peace justice stewardship speak to your condition

ARE YOU READY FOR CHRISTMAS?

"Are you ready for Christmas?" I don't know where that saying comes from, but if Christmas is about love and peace, how can one not be ready for it?

The phrase evokes mad shopping dashes to malls, ripped wrapping paper, and faked surprises for presents—wanted and not. For me, "Are you ready for Christmas?" translates to: "Have you bought my present yet?"

When I was growing up, Santa had restrictions. The chimney was off limits, and Santa was allowed to bring one present only. A pair of freshly-shined boots waited for him inside the double-pane window of the mud-brick house.

Conflicted by "modern" Christmas, I had tried, every year, to fight off the cultural divide by ignoring it. But one year, succumbing to the pressure, I decided to play by the "rules."

As my luck goes, the very first person I dared to query about "Christmas readiness" happened to be the wrong guy. "For me," he said "every day is Christmas."

Since then, I have learned that early Friends rejected the celebration of Christmas as well. Celebrating love and peace on a special day somehow implies that on all other days they don't matter that much.

"Every day is Christmas" says one needs no presents or riches to live life in love and peace.

You can and you may conduct your life by the way of the Light and the Spirit—every day.

THIS LITTLE LIGHT OF MINE

I have been thinking about a Friend who departed from us. At Marie's service, a friend spoke of her as "the little old lady." That, in fact, was the way I knew Marie.

By the time I arrived at meeting, Marie was frail, her voice faint, and she walked very slowly in tiny steps. In her long discolored coat and with her long white hair she looked like a floating angel.

Suddenly, at the service, a woman began to sing: "This little Light of mine, I'm gonna let it shine..." There was Marie, in that song. That song was precisely about her.

Marie had never let her physical condition deter her. If she had something to say, she would say it. And she wanted everybody to be like her.

One Sunday, I caught up with Marie on the way to the car. She said to me off the cuff: "Why don't more people speak in meeting? They must be thinking *something*!"

Speaking one's mind takes conviction, but above all, it takes courage. How do we learn them? The best way, perhaps the only way, is by having role models. Marie was one of mine in both—conviction *and* courage.

Marie had been one of the "old-timers" in town. Those who had known her spoke of the many ways Marie had touched their lives.

For me, the new kid on the block, to be among them was unexpected. And yet, there I was. I was there because...

It takes but a second to be touched by an angel

86

DAVE'S VISION

Dave lives in a two-hundred-year-old farmhouse. He feels more like the steward than the owner of this gem, merely nursing it with love until the next occupant will take over the chain of care. He feels gratitude to be a part of that continuity.

Dave is part of another admirable process—the revival of an old meeting house in his town.

Dave has the vision that one day this meeting house will become another gem, a quiet oasis adorned by a peaceful, well-attended garden ready to invite the world to witness the Spirit inside.

His vision will not materialize overnight. A vision is only the first step in a slow process. Many challenging steps must be overcome.

Vision can only materialize if sustained by faith in its worthiness and by staying the course regardless of the obstacles.

Our own meeting house has stood for two hundred years and will likely stand for two hundred more. It has witnessed many momentous events, and will witness many more down the road.

In midst of turmoil, it has always stood as a place of solace and spiritual refuge. It has always stood and will stand for noble, commendable values.

Being a link in the chain of its praiseworthy life is as rewarding as the stewardship of Dave's farmhouse and garden of the Spirit.

WHO NEEDS A TREE?

The last time I saw him, John Harvey was speaking in meeting for worship. John was intensely angry. His ire was aimed at the Society of Friends for its glut of words and lack of action.

Those were John's departing words. He died shortly after. John was fifty-four years of age. A rock in my garden carries John's name. I think of his message each and every time I walk by. I took John's words personally.

Friends in meeting have been contemplating a memorial tree for John. Did John want a tree bearing his name? I don't know, but I do know the best way to honor John's memory and what he stood for is through our actions.

Better yet, in this day and age, when nouns become verbs overnight, when one can google, friend, and facebook, let us coin a word for John—a word of action.

Let harvey mean to follow the leadings of the Spirit above and beyond our comfort zone. When roadblocks dim our vision and snag our resolve, a gentle nudge—a harvey—will come to rescue. Let the inevitable triumph of the Spirit be our harvey moment.

John Harvey is my hero. He is my hero for his principles and his resolve. Above all, he is my hero for his courage to stand firm by those principles, regardless of the consequences; regardless of people's opinions of him.

John's message is with me every day, as I confront my own misgivings.

John Harvey is much on my mind this Memorial Day

REWARDS

Last week, I "overheard" a conversation between Jesus and his disciples: "He who receives you," Jesus said, "Receives me, and he who receives me receives the one who sent me."

"He who receives a prophet will get the prophet's reward, and he who receives a righteous man will receive the righteous man's reward. He who gives even a glass of cold water to the lowliest will not lose his reward."

If Jesus were here amongst us he would surely say "there is that of God in everyone," just to please Quakers.

That is the exact reason why I like to talk to *all* the people I meet. Every single one is a reflection of the whole world—just a slightly different rendition of color and hue. Every single one is God's image and wisdom.

Talking to strangers is as easy as offering them a glass of cold water.

And the reward? What is the reward? What is the reward for meeting and receiving God in His infinite iterations?

Receiving the prophet is rewarded by the prophet's reward. Receiving the righteous man is rewarded by the reward of the righteous man.

The reward is like the action itself. Receiving God is receiving God's reward.

Receiving a prophet means gaining his presence, his wisdom, and his example. So it is with the wisdom and presence in doing God's work. Doing God's work is the very reward for doing so.

GOT SUCCESS?

Our Friend Doug wove levity into his spiritual life in enigmatic ways. His vocal ministry was thoughtful yet distinctly anecdotal. At the rise of meeting, it was Doug invariably whipping up laughter with anyone who happened to come his way.

It was Doug who posed the thought-provoking dilemma: "What's more important, peace or justice? You can't have both." Who would have guessed that Friends noble testimonies may actually conflict one another?

Doug came over for a visit one day to "sit on the deck with a few beers and...tell lies." It was the end of summer, and I was smarting from losses in my garden. It had been a rough season. Whole stretches of plants withered without apparent reason. The very character of the garden was changing. Maybe Doug didn't know that.

But he quickly looked around and blurted: "Do you have successes in your garden?" Sure I had successes. The mimosa I grew from seed had shot up an incredible eight feet in the previous months. I was in awe of it every time I walked by. And my long-planned wisteria tree had at last acquired the mushroom shape it was meant to have.

Doug's question has permanently shifted my way of thinking. It was a life-changing proposition. What's done is done. Simple logic implies that any garden will suffer damage at some point. Keeping score just doesn't make sense. Seeking successes, though, is a window into the future.

Anticipating success is a gift of continuing revelation

ANCESTORS

Mulan is the young heroine of an eponymous film. Her country is in mortal danger of enemy invasion, and Mulan is considering unprecedented action. She will become a soldier. She will serve and defend her country as a man. But Mulan needs help.

Ancestor worship is central to many Eastern cultures, and ultimately, it will be her ancestors' decision. Mulan performs the ancestor-awakening ritual to seek their counsel. Accordingly, she becomes a soldier. She saves her country from invasion and becomes a heroine.

The meeting family has its ancestors. They are the Friends who, for many years, had worshipped here, shared their enlightenment, and left a legacy of wisdom and empowerment.

I can think of many, but Paul comes to mind. It is perhaps because Paul sat in front of me in the same spot, week after week, year after year. We shook hands at the rise of every meeting, every Sunday.

Paul and his generation seem to surround me in support. I feel they lift me up higher. Their presence makes me taller and stronger, more determined, and spiritually more empowered.

Our own presence in worship serves the same purpose.

We bestow our personal strengths and the wisdom we have gained through the Light to a new generation of Friends.

And thus, by our presence, we impart and perpetuate the lessons of Paul and the others who came before us.

91

SINNER LITE

Two men brought a paralytic before Jesus. "Take heart son," Jesus said, "Your sins are forgiven. Get up and go home." And the man did.

The scribes weren't happy. The fellow had sinned. He deserved to be paralyzed. What right did Jesus have to upend that order? What right did he have to heal him? His remark "I come for the sinners; the healthy need no doctor" was disturbing to them.

What could that poor guy have done? For a sin like murder or for breaking the Sabbath he would have long been stoned. Had his sin been the sin of Adam, the whole town would have been in wheelchairs.

His "sin" had to be the breaking of a rule made by the scribes themselves. Punishment proved their rule right. It upheld their order and their hegemony.

But who has the right to take away the God-given life-sustaining energy that supports health and happiness? Who has authority over the Inner Light?

"All sins are forgiven," Jesus says, for they are merely human failings. A sinner is one who merely stumbled, one who lost his way. That "sinner-lite" may only need guidance to do better the next time.

"I desire mercy not burnt sacrifices" is a call upon Friends as ministers to do what Friends do best:

Hold in the Light

Steer to the Light

EXETER BICENTENNIAL

Friends who gather here weekly are accustomed to this room. Rarely if ever do they think about the past. For an infrequent visitor like me, it echoes centuries of Quaker life. The inordinately thick walls be may be the sole reason.

The nearby Boone Homestead fleshes out that history with artifacts and reenactments. This bicentennial celebration certainly adds to it.

Most striking to me is the graveyard outside this building. It has been long dormant. Its graves are layered, devoid of markers, shrouded in anonymity.

They convey a sense of finality to the lives of the Friends who worshipped here. As the meeting fell silent a hundred years ago, it seems as if all matters were tidied up and put away. The meeting house stayed in its hibernation for fifty years.

But the message I hear today seems to say:

"We were here. We lived here, worshipped here, and we created this meeting house for you.

We left a rich history and a solid legacy. Our job was done, and now we are gone. You have received a gift—a new clean, slate. It is now up to you what to do next.

What will you do with this legacy? Where will you take it from here? It is up to you."

It is a powerful message from the past

It is a message full of inspiration and responsibility

A LAB UNENCUMBERED

Two Friends have joined us recently—life-long seekers who have found in meeting a promising spiritual home.

Meeting has no doctrines or hired clergy. It only has one thing: continuing revelation. Because of that, perhaps, meeting can offer something no one else can: an unencumbered spiritual laboratory with transformative powers. Being its product, I know.

*   *

Given the option, I would have picked the fast track to Quakerism, say a Quaker pill of which you take two and wake up Quaker in the morning. Still, twenty years later, I am here as I am in good measure because of that lab.

The plain version of the transformation, one may say, is seeing the Light. And that is good news, better than what all the noisy evangelists could come up with together.

Our new Friends have reminded me of that. They have reminded me of the awesome spiritual potential meeting has. To that I will speak far and wide.

Doing the work of meeting or writing a check are some of the ways to give back. But the best way is just to come here and sit.

Through our worshipful presence, we create the spiritual space for the lab and grow its powers of transformation.

So here I am, for our new Friends and for all others, with my humble presence and my two square feet of spiritual space.

FROM DUTY OR LOVE

In *Love at First Sight,* a young man miraculously regains his vision. Sight opens new and exciting worlds for him, but soon, he regrets the miracle. He learns to see the ills of the world. Having been oblivious to all that pain before, he comes to believe he had been better off without his sight.

Kids are born free spirits. They play as their hearts desire and do what they want to do. In time, they see good and bad, learn right from wrong, and learn to choose doing what is right. As adults, they carry out those duties whether they want to or not. But does that matter?

Does it matter if we do what we do out of duty or out of love? Once you paid your taxes, does the IRS care why you did? What about human affairs?

As every person reflects *all* of God's Creation, is getting to know someone duty or privilege? Does it matter if human interactions are or are not the result of love?

Does it matter if someone is nice, friendly, or civil out of duty or because they want to be? Must one ever doubt the motive?

*   *

As I weighed these dilemmas in the wake of personal encounters, Cica, my cat showed up.

> He jumped instantly into my lap and with
> typical enthusiasm made himself noticed

> There was no need to question his motives
> Purring from the heart gave away his unquestionable love

BRING IT OUT

The ocean of my childhood had knee-deep golden sand and cobalt-like navy blue water. Late-day thunderstorms left picture-perfect rainbows and giant fluffy clouds in their wake, bursting with the colors of the setting sun.

I wish everything were as vivid as those cherished memories of mine. I still use purple sunglasses to look at sunsets and fall colors. The tinted glass brings out details you do not see with the naked eye.

My Facebook friends think I use Photoshop. I don't, and I don't know if Photoshop can create color. I can't. I can only enhance what already is there. I can only amplify it. I was told I obsessed with color-saturation. Indeed, I was doing just that. I was amplifying the color.

As we are unable to hear wave signals, we use TV's and radios to amplify them. No one can hear what the Spirit channels through me unless I amplify it and bring out the message in words.

Being a human amplifier is an intriguing thought—a selective amplifier, that is. The state of the world rests on the deeds of the people. A selective amplifier makes a karmic filter that grows the good and holds back the bad.

To save the world, one need not necessarily be an inventor of good, only a channeller of it.

As violence breeds violence, kindness returns kindness. Work can be done by virtue of example.

Jesus calls it working for the Kingdom

JOYS OF THE SPIRIT

Meetings as ours have no hired ministers. We are all ministers who bring our gifts and talents to serve the community. A Friend said there is an office to everyone; everyone is of service.

A recent article elaborates on the joys of ministry. Sharing one's gifts, it says, is a central motif of Quakerism, and sharing one's gifts to benefit others is a joyful experience.

*   *

I ask this morning: Is worship itself a joyous experience?

The essence of worship is the same: settle our minds and open our hearts to the Divine. Worship varies only because Friends receive different leadings from week to week.

Sharing the leadings of the Spirit is joyful to me

Worship is an exercise in self-empowerment. Channeling the Divine gives us domain over what enters our minds. To that end, we carve out a niche of time each week and create a sacred laboratory.

Taking part in that exercise is joyful to me

Over time, the thoughts we allow into our minds shape our character and define who we are. Becoming a person closer to God's image is a noble pursuit and a worthy spiritual destination.

That journey is joyful to me

WHAT DO YOU THINK?

Everything is asleep in my garden now, except the squirrels. They run, dig, and climb and run some more. Then, unexpectedly, they freeze as if stunned. A "Quaker moment" perhaps? My Quaker moment came as a new Friend asked: "Why do you want to be a Quaker?"

That is a very, very good question. "What do Quakers believe in?" is another. As much as Friends dread it, the answer to it is quite simple: everything! To any given question a hundred Friends will have as many answers.

Friends also have good clichés. "You've been a Quaker but didn't know it" is among my favorites. No one should be surprised that seekers bring with them values as peace, simplicity, and spirituality which they want to be affirmed.

We may hear "What brings you to Quakerism?" In the hubbub of the moment, it was what entered my mind. So, I told the new Friend about a 1980 peace poster and praised the simplicity of my friend's Quaker wedding—my first real spiritual experience.

Since then, I have learned a couple of things. I have learned that the "everyone" in "the Light of God in everyone" includes me! It means that I am as good and worthy as everyone else; not better, just good.

I can now also say that I am the sum-total of everything that ever happened in the Universe—every star, gene, and smile. Those are powerful messages.

Or take continuing revelation, which to me, means that there will always be something to inspire me—something to give me purpose.

Those are life-changing lessons enough for a lifetime. But they are in the past. I could write a thank you note to the Clerk and move on. Why do I want to be a Quaker *now*? That question brought clarity as never before.

In the wake of a tenuous exchange with my lawyer friend about God, I treaded lightly in my "spiritual" talk with my scientist friend. Even though I had sought common ground, nothing I said seemed to speak to his condition.

Finally, I asked: Why do you think what *do* you think? After a Quaker moment of his own, he blurted: "I have no idea!" In fact, what does or does not pop into our minds at any moment of time is out of our hands.

Imagine a hospital scene in a Spanish film. A nurse is comforting a dying patient: "Do you want to watch TV?" "No, I have to think," he says. "What do you think about," she asks. "That isn't for me to decide!" That was a stunning Quaker moment, and it has stayed with me to this day.

Thinking, it dawned on me, is not only the most essential privilege of life, but what we do or do not think and why is at the very core of Quakerism. In worship, we quiet our minds and still our hearts to hear the truth of the Divine. Sharing that truth, we call ministry.

"Spiritual beehive" is my best metaphor for meeting. Like honeybees darting from flower to flower, Friends seek the truth everywhere they go. On First Days, they share their spiritual nectar. Worship creates a sacred space for it, and by virtue that space, meeting empowers ministry.

How do you explain all that in five nanoseconds? Since people do understand "Cash & Carry" and "Park & Ride," I got me a bumper sticker! "Be a Quaker, Thinker Maker."

JACOB AND THE ANGEL

A Friend spoke of words and their meaning as he reflected on Quakers' treaty with the Indians in their new colony. The Quakers understood the treaty to mean purchasing the land. To the Indians it meant sharing it.

Words may mean different things even to people of the same culture and language. But the quarrel with the Indians wasn't even about semantics but concept. In the world of the Indians, land, as air, couldn't be bought or owned.

My thoughts drifted to a different confusion, one also rooted in a cultural gap—a two-thousand-year-old gap. That gap becomes evident in reading the Bible and trying to make sense of phrases filled with angels, evil spirits, and heavenly kingdoms.

Looking at the ancient Bible with modern eyes leads to bewildering conclusions. In that vein, Jacob's wrestling the angel is one of the most bizarre stories in the book.

"Jacob was left alone, and there wrestled a man until the break of the day. Thy name shall be called no more Jacob, but Israel, for hast thou power with God and with men, and hast prevailed."

The story can make sense, though, if we simply allow for the angel to be Jacob's conscience. On the eve of confronting Esau, his wronged brother, Jacob faced his past, his fears, and his penance.

He spent the night in worship, discerning the right thing to do. Jacob chose the higher spiritual ground. The way of the Kingdom prevailed. Jacob got a new name to reflect God's way: Israel.

QUERIES OF NOVEMBER

Queries have been Friends way to examine the state of their affairs since the days of William Penn.

Queries have evolved over the centuries.

Each generation finds its own voice and adopts its concerns to reflect prevailing conditions in society.

Currently, there are twelve queries, each with its own rambling and exhaustive detail.

Focusing the query process on just two or three items may enable Friends to indeed ask and answer them.

*   *

This month's Queries probe the stewardship of resources—material and spiritual ones alike.

Of the spiritual resources, time is the most precious one
Therefore, as Friends, let us ask and answer

Do my engagements at large allow time for
spiritual growth and service in the Society of Friends?

To meeting, Friends are the most precious resource
Therefore, as a corporate body, let us ask and answer

What does meeting do to support Friends in their
spiritual ministry and work of the meeting?

101

STEWARDSHIP 101

My thoughts, this morning, are on stewardship. Friends are proud stewards of everything under the sun, from the Earth to meeting resources. But Friends rarely include themselves in their concerns or look into the most precious resource of all—life itself.

Friend Francis used to say: "There is no light without darkness." Does that mean we cannot fully cherish peace without war? Must we "Live as we were dying" in order to value life to the fullest?

There are no stewardship queries about life, even though we could contemplate questions as:

Do you have a master plan for your life?

What will you do with your life today?

"Blessed art thou who giveth life who has sustained us and has brought us to this day" is my all-time favorite blessing.

I painted a caption onto a rock in my garden as a reminder to ask every day:

What will I do with my new day's gift of life?

Worship, Friends most valued endeavor, can be a reminder of the stewardship of our most valuable asset—life itself.

So tonight, Friends can try a new query:

Have I used today's gift of life to my satisfaction?

I AIN'T SLEEPIN'—A TRIBUTE TO MY CAT

On the surface, it may look as if Cica's favorite thing in the world is sleep.

I am not talking about the frequent occasions of total oblivion when his majesty seems to have abandoned his terrestrial body.

It is the endless stretches in the day that I have in mind, interrupted only by a quick meal, when he "sleeps" in the morning sun or a shady hideout in the afternoon.

Closed eyes don't necessarily mean sleep. Anyone who has seen Quaker worship will tell you that. Hopefully, Quakers don't sleep in their worship too often. They are said to be "in the Spirit." What exactly that means is a different story.

My Cica may have the answer

As Quakers' claim to hear things in silence that no one else can, Cica's own abilities confound the human mind.

Cica needs his vision only to confirm his ready-made assessments assembled from olfactory and auditory minutiae inconceivable to humans.

His triple-decked ears, white whiskers, and pink nose sense every bird, bug, and fur-ball hundreds of feet away.

He is in unison with the rustle of every leaf and the passing of every cloud, the faintest of breezes and the slightest whiff of aroma. He is in communion with his world.

No, he ain't sleeping…He is in the Spirit

HOW FAR WILL YOU GO?

Absent today are a number of Friends who departed from us lately. But we are joined by a week-old new Friend. It is the cycle of life that we recognize and accept.

"As we near the end of this cycle, we make conscious preparations for our departure. It isn't a sad time, only one phase of the cycle." These words were spoken by an elderly Friend.

Another form of preparation is a continuous effort to live a life that leaves no regrets. That means a fulfilled, joyful, and inspired life.

I have the greatest admiration for the coaches who enable such life: school teachers and spiritual teachers, Friendly mentors and nurturers, and all the others whom we encounter in our spiritual journey.

Nothing, however, can surpass the act of saving a life. For that reason, I view Gregory House—the good doctor from *House, MD*—as a hero. His only motivation is "to do the right thing," the often talked about Quaker ideal.

Dr. House will go to any extreme to save a life, be it lying to the family, defying a court order, or exhuming a dead rat.

Most of us will never encounter opportunities or challenges of such magnitude. Still, Doctor House's example is an inspiration for all.

We do face dilemmas large and small

How far are we willing to go to do the right thing?

IN SEARCH OF A PROJECT

We all have the need to do something. We seek direction and purpose. We need a project to bring meaning to our lives. And what can be more meaningful than coaching someone reach their life-potential?

It is a life-long project. You must learn everything about the person: their joys and sorrows, their powers and ambitions—the very things that make them tick.

You must be a cheerleader for their work. You must amuse and elate them. You must inspire them and expand their minds, nourish their souls and uplift their spirits.

Whether you are a parent or a friend, a spiritual nurturer, or simply an ordinary Quaker minister, you are doing no one a favor except yourself. You must be grateful for the chance to gain purpose.

*   *

Mother was a beautiful, bright, and ambitious teen. At sixteen, the world she had known came to an end. Her ambitions remained a dream. She felt failure in career and in love. Intellectually unfulfilled, her soul ran on empty.

Yet, unbeknown to her, she had done the most important job in the world, and she had done it better than anyone I know. She was a mother. My mother.

"I live my life for you," she used to say. Of all the things she ever said, that burdening sacrifice I hated the most. "Thank you for giving me purpose," however, would have made me feel the most important person in the world.

PRINCIPLES ON DEATH ROW

There are two doctors. Both are at the top of their profession. Both are driven by idealistic devotion and view their vocation as ministry.

One doctor has worked in the farthest corners of Africa in deplorable conditions. He saved the lives of thousands, perhaps tens of thousands of patients. He is a hero.

His colleague is a top diagnostician. He will go to extremes to treat all his patients regardless of their circumstances. He saved the lives of hundreds of patients whom no other doctor could help.

One such patient is a six-foot-five death-row inmate, three hundred pounds of solid muscle. He may only leave his solitary confinement in handcuffs. While on death-row, he had killed a guard, an inmate, and the librarian who dared to look at him.

Hours before his execution, the doctor transfers the inmate to the hospital and finds a rare tumor—the source of all the rage and violence. The "real" man is an intelligent, introspective, and caring individual. The death sentence is appealed.

Which doctor is the greater hero?

Which one works for the greater good?

Justice is a fundamental Quaker value and the foundation on which this country rests.

If death-row inmates are expendable before the law
others will soon follow

JUSTICE OR VENGEANCE

A provocative program on the death penalty was presented today. Concerns were weighed on moral, spiritual, and financial grounds. The deterrent value was questioned. Fallibility and fairness were debated.

What struck a chord with me the most was whether the death penalty strives to achieve justice or vengeance. A film comes to mind with a dramatized parallel.

The victim of a heinous crime, distraught beyond reasoning by the experience, could no longer tell the line between justice and vengeance. Only the chaos that followed the victim's vengeance revealed the difference.

Friends peace testimony rests on religious and spiritual grounds. As there is that of God in everyone, nothing can justify taking that life. And as the testimony says, the Spirit Jesus is not changeable to command us away from evil and again back to it.

Not all Friends agree with that, but no one disputes the fact that violence begets more violence. In the world today, revenge for fifty car-bomb victims leads to a hundred more.

Chaos does only one thing. In a downward spiral, it devalues human life. In war, its value is nil. We, Americans, have not experienced that in our midst. Even so, when a young man is willing to kill a store keeper, or a cop, or lose his own life for thirty dollars, we are close to it.

That young man's desperation rests on the shoulders of society. Restoring the value of his life would be a show of justice.

A LESSON FROM TREES

Much thought goes into the charms of the seasons. Undeniably, spring's burst of color and fragrance appeals to most. Spring brings joyful expectancy and hope. But tensions arrive with them. Future storms must be weathered and the battles of life must be won.

Fall brings calm. The battles have been fought, the lessons have been learned. Choices have been made and their aftermath accepted. In fall, wisdom supplants innocence, knowledge makes whole. There is solace in fall—a sense of reward. In the fall of my own life, I choose fall.

Trees too follow the annual cycle of life. They come alive in spring with tender leaves prepared to absorb the energy of the summer sun. In fall, as their work is done, the leaves don glorious colors before they fall off and die.

This life-cycle is deeply spiritual for me. As dead as trees may look in winter time, come spring, they awaken to life once more. The annual renewal puts the biblical death-and-resurrection into a whole new light to consider.

The dramatic cycle that trees follow year in and year out is their adaptation to existing conditions of light and heat. Unlike people who do at times, trees do not question their appearance or their whereabouts in that process.

Trees have not only made me accept my place in my own life-cycle but have taught me a valuable choice. I can choose to look at my life either as the life of the leaves or the life of the trees. I choose the latter.

A chain of life renewed in each generation

SMALL STEPS FORWARD

"Elijah will come first and mend all things," says the passage in Matthew 17:11. "But he has come already," comments Jesus, "And he was not recognized by the people."

Do we recognize the Elijahs in our lives? Do we acknowledge the things in our lives that have been mended?

Do we recognize our opportunities to set things right for others and for the so called Kingdom?

Without much thought, most people work conscientiously to make things better for them and for others. Work for the Kingdom consists of many small opportunities.

*   *

No power in Heaven or on Earth, they say, can move humanity forward if people don't embrace the idea and work toward it.

Technology today has given unprecedented power to the people. I can now make things better for many by simply retelling my own story.

I have had two experiences this week with car people — one very good, the other very bad. It is my chance to mend something. I will now write two reviews online—one very good and one very bad.

The good dealership is thriving. Perhaps the good reviews on their website—feedback from satisfied customers—have been the reason.

OF SPIRITS AND RESURRECTION

A biblical Jewish law dictates that when one brother dies another brother must marry the widow and raise children in the deceased's name.

The Sadducees, who did not believe in resurrection, try to trip Jesus with seven brothers who had died instead of one. "Who is married to whom," they ask, "when all are resurrected?" "The resurrected are like the angels in Heaven," Jesus explains, "and not like men who take wives."

"I am the God of Abraham, Isaac, and Jacob," God tells Moses at the burning bush. Abraham, Isaac, and Jacob had been dead for a long time, but "God is the God of the living not of the dead." God is the God of Abraham, Isaac, and Jacob because they are alive in Spirit.

I think of bygone Friends who worshipped here and generously shared their wisdom and enlightenment. I still hear their voices and often recall their messages. They still play an active role in my life. While no longer here in body, they are very much here in Spirit.

I think of my dear mother, who has been gone for over half of my life. Her voice has faded and her memory becomes more distant with each passing year. But her Spirit lives in me. All her love and the goodness of her heart have taken deep roots in my soul.

Even though faraway, I feel as if, like a guardian angel, her presence still watches over me.

From the inside of my soul she continues to give me subtle guidance and reassuring protection.

SIN—SNOW—AND MINISTRY

Eskimos have twenty words for snow. English has more, and some are good ones like pillow-drift and watermelon, not to mention snirt—the portmanteau of snow and dirt. In spite of the variety, we only use one: snow. It starts with "S," is monosyllabic, and packs a punch.

There may be a good reason for it. Imagine an ill-conceived consumption of a Zastrugi cone or the popularity drop of the national pastime of building hoar men. I dare not speculate the aftermath of a misdirected dendrite ball.

Even more choice exists with transgression. Centuries of human misery notwithstanding, and to my dismay, once again, we use only "sin." The reasons are the same. Sin is monosyllabic, starts with "S," and is the easiest to say.

Recourse arrived from unexpected corners: my advanced Arabic class. There, in the comparative religion section, I found not one, or two, but three different kinds of sins. My excitement turned "sin" into my final thesis.

The worst sins are about desire: lust to be in another place and another time, gluttony for more than needed, and greed for more of everything. Sloth is about doing nothing. Wrath is about hatred, and envy is the hatred for what others have but we don't. Pride is the desire to be more than others and the root of all sins.

They mean nothing, though, for Jesus himself said that all sins are forgiven—all except the sin against the Holy Spirit. What that may be is in the realm of mystery. Friends view that the Holy Spirit—the Light—resides inside narrows down the mystery but raises the onus to find an answer. What is the unforgivable sin against the Light?

Dismissing one's Light and stymying one's calling are sins that should never happen. But Friends tend to forget their own Light. And here is the special challenge. What is the unforgivable sin against one's own Light, the special God-given gifts and talents that make each person one of a kind?

Of the above seven "deadliest" sins, I venture to claim that intellectual, but above all, spiritual sloth is the unforgivable sin. One may argue with aspects of my choice, but if you wasted your gifts and talents, you wasted the only life you had. How can that be forgiven?

*   *

My all-time favorite Friendly phrase is: "Shine your Light for others to love." Shining your Light simply means sharing your God-given gifts and inspiration with others; in Friends words—ministry.

My Arabic class was small, at times just over a handful of students. Josh was one. Josh had a learning disability and often talked about his challenges to do academic work. But Josh had never missed a class. In class Josh made the most thoughtful and astute observations.

I made my presentation for him. As I spoke, I looked directly at him. I wanted him to know how important his efforts were. I wanted him to materialize his potential, to keep going and not to give up. Did he get the message? I hope he did. I really do. But had he not, I would have still done my presentation. Do you know why? Because:

This little light of mine, I'm gonna let it shine
Everywhere I go, I'm gonna let it shine
All around the world, I'm gonna let it shine
Let it shine, let it shine, let it shine…

SIMPLE REWARDS

My English-major daughter called me from college one day: "Dad," she said, "I love science! In a world of ambiguities, it gives me something firm to rely on." In a twist of irony, an English major found solace in Science.

Our meeting house is a place of solace, especially on a bright spring morning when the giant cherry tree is in full bloom. Here, for a short time, the hubbub of the world gives way to a sacred space of spiritual peace.

In high school, algebra was *my* solace. The jumble of figures held a secret. With a few tricks, those mind-boggling pages dissolved into something skeletal like X=1. There was beauty in those pages, a unique form of craftsmanship. One generation later, X became 1.33, and Math devolved into a skill for using calculators.

Few kids born today will ever see an old-fashioned sewing machine, let alone absorb the undulating rhythm of its treadle. I can still feel the heft of my ancient solid-brass mortar-and-pestle. I can hear its resonant clanking. I can still feel the kick of the keys on my manual typewriter as on the day I typed my first resume on it.

Old tools were made in the simplest way, to do the job the simplest way. Simplicity gets into the blood. Once you have experienced it, you come to expect it and demand it. Simplicity leads to the essence of things. Much is to be learned from it about nature and about ourselves.

Yet, even the simplest X=1 leaves us with a fundamental problem. We may know that X=1, but we don't know what X is. *We* must provide the contents. It is up to *us* to find meaning.

113

In Friendly Bible Study we search for X in five steps:
What is the main point of the passage?
What is the new light?
Is it true to my experience?
What implications apply to my life?
What problems do I see?

New light reflects continuing revelation. The subsequent steps query relevance to our condition. But the crux of the search is in step one. What is X? In the simplest and the starkest terms, the search for X is the search for the truth.

Matthew 10:40 is a verbose and cryptic passage. A bit of parsing, though, strips the passage to two words: "everybody" and "reward." Biblical reward usually means something big like salvation or eternal life. Here, Jesus says no such thing. It is a simple deal: everyone who plays gets a reward.

A close look reveals that the reward is like the effort. He who receives the prophet will receive the prophet's reward; he who receives the righteous will get the reward of the righteous, and will benefit from their wisdom, their enlightenment, and their presence. In other words, the reward is the work itself.

I first heard this concept at a Friends event. It registered instantly as a deeply significant tenet, at the root of all human endeavors. It explains everything that we do in our daily lives as citizens and Friends, and in our spiritual lives as members of Downingtown Friends Meeting.

It explains why Jesus focused on his ministry and rejected publicity and acclaim. It may also explain why—for the most part—Friends are reluctant to applaud or receive recognition.

114

THE FRIENDLY BIBLE

More often than not, the Bible is read for affirmation of values and beliefs. What is the Quaker way of doing that?

Jesus came to fill the Law with the Spirit and to renew it to reflect the condition of his generation. His ministry of love *is* Friends guiding light in their search for affirmation.

The Sermon on the Mount is the start of that ministry and sets the stage for all the other teachings. It begins with counsel to turn the other cheek but ends with the admonition to become perfected as God is: pure and complete, enlightened and holy.

Jesus blesses the poor in Spirit—all who are pure at heart but burn with longings and are prepared to do something about them. "Blessed are the poor in Spirit" is meant for all those who seek God's path to the Light and the Spirit.

The meek of the sermon harbor no anger, malice, or a need for revenge. They do stand their ground firmly, however, empowered by their God-given inalienable rights. With them, are those thirsty for justice and the blessed workers for peace—the carriers of the Quaker testimonies banner.

"Love your enemy" may be the most radical of Jesus's teachings. But Friends know that violence begets more violence, and that he who sows hatred, sooner than later, reaps hatred. What if "love your enemy" simply means sowing no hatred?

"Love your enemy" is stopping violence—one step at a time. In Jesus's ministry, the Kingdom of Heaven is a place where all work together toward one goal. In that world, all grievances are seen to, and no one harbors hatred.

BLESSED ARE THE POOR IN SPIRIT

"Poor in Spirit" in the Sermon on the Mount has been read in many ways. Gabriella, in the film *As It Is In Heaven*, tells it best. It is about her strife for spiritual renewal; her desire to live her life to the fullest in God's Creation.

> All I lacked and had to gain
> My longing has brought me here
> My trust was far beyond words
> in the Heaven I haven't yet found
>
> I want to be strong and free
> I want to feel I lived my life
> I want to see day arise from night
>
> I want to be happy with who I am
> To live my life knowing I was good enough

Gabriella seeks spiritual transformation to break away from the past. She seeks to connect with her Inner Light.

"Live my life knowing I was good enough" strikes the loudest chord with me. I hear the empowerment to follow one's calling, to know it was what needed to be done.

In lieu of spending a lifetime trying to do what others may like, say: "This is what I do. I hope you like it." That is to say: "I shine my Light for others to love."

According to George Fox:

> The Light that shines in the heart of a man
> Is the Light that was shining when the world began
> With a book and a steeple and a bell and a key
> Many would bind it forever but they can't—said he

116

GLOB NO MORE

A young mother has just converted to creationism.

She *had* believed that life evolved from simple chemical compounds but had trouble telling her nine-year-old son that he was a glob of protoplasm.

To me, the beauty of life on Earth offers plenty of marvels, and so, I have no use for that debate. But there is a hitch.

Random evolution not only implies happenstance but a lack of purpose to everything that exists. To me, that *is* a problem.

Logically thinking, creation of man and evolution of man cannot be both right, for there is only one man.

The Bible tells us that God formed Adam—the first man—"out of the dust of the earth and breathed the breath of life into his nostrils and he became a living being."

The biblical "dust of the earth" may have been our ancient glob. By breathing the Spirit into his nostril, God made Adam the first human being.

In this picture, the world did not begin six thousand years ago but had existed forever. Six thousand years ago, God blew human awareness into Adam's nostrils.

Thus, Adam was not the first man on Earth. Millions had lived before him. Adam was the first human capable of probing the purpose of his own existence.

It is a scenario that may just please everyone, and the young mother may still say "glob" to get her son's attention.

117

LET NO MAN SEPARATE

At Mount Sinai, Moses was summoned to receive God's plan for His people. The people, however, had made plans of their own, and upon return, Moses was met with the Golden Calf. The Golden Calf has been the greatest blasphemy against God, ever since.

That story came to mind at a reading, where Jesus probes matters of divorce. In that faraway world, Abraham—the man of God—could buy multiple wives and concubines, and on a whim, cast them into the desert to certain death. Laws of that world cannot possibly apply today.

But Jesus didn't go to laws for answers. He went to the very beginning. "Male and female the Creator made them," he said "to unite them and become one flesh. What God joined together let no one separate." As such, God's Creation is the first and the final word.

That recognition has far-reaching implications for body and soul, for it puts all man's deeds under the magnifying glass. The Golden Calf may have been allegorical, but all that man has himself made since Creation is as arrogant as the idol itself.

Everything that man does to the Earth and to his God-created body needs careful scrutiny. All that man puts into his mind and soul should reflect God's work. Man's laws and brainstorms need to follow the primeval truth and the facts of Creation.

God's Creation is an inherent right of all humankind. Let no man deny the air, the water, or the sunshine that God created. Let no man jeopardize the bounty of the Earth that God made as only He knew how.

A MATTER OF WORDS

As sister languages, Hebrew and Arabic share a multitude of word stems. Over time, such words are likely to assume divergent nuances. But Arabic exhibits a remarkable trend that elevates the meanings of words, reflecting cultural progress and the maturing of society.

The most striking example, perhaps, is the word "ya'e." It means dustpan in the former and conscience in the latter. Both suggest actions of collection—a kind of convergence perhaps—dust on one hand, awareness and reason on the other.

It is a parallel to the biblical birth of Adam. God gathered dust and formed the body of Adam. Then he blew the Spirit into his nostrils endowing him with awareness and with the power of reason that made Adam a human being.

*   *

The analogy came in handy as I wrestled with the passage in Matthew that, for the first time, raises the matter of eternal life. What does eternal life mean, and how does it relate to entering the Kingdom of Heaven?

"Keep the commandments," Jesus says, "But he who wants to be perfected must follow me." Then it clicked. Jesus speaks of his teachings as spiritual awaking—from dust to man. Blowing the Spirit into Adam is the perfect metaphor.

Spiritual awaking means eternal life. It means awareness and understanding of the Kingdom and its principles. It reveals the ways to work toward it. "Entering the Kingdom" is just another way of saying the same thing.

SPIRITUAL RITUALS

Rituals are religious procedures. That much is clear. But what is spirituality? It could be said that spirituality is a search for who we are and who we are called to be.

Rituals and spirituality complement each other in puzzling ways. Is there a dimension of spirituality in all rituals? Are rituals part of spirituality as in "spi-ritual," or is it a bit of both?

We may think of spirituality in terms of the goals we are aspiring to. Being brave, strong, and wise are good goals to aim for, as are all the others that may excite and inspire us. Rituals, on the other hand, bring forth the vision, courage, and fortitude to overcome the obstacles on the way.

The question is: Are there good rituals and bad rituals?

The Pharisees, for example, were so immersed in rituals that they lost sight of goals. "You understand the appearance of the sky," Jesus tells them, "but not the signs of the times." The Pharisees lost touch with the Spirit.

They lost touch with reality. Friends may say they lost of the Inner Light. I venture to say they lost their divine intuition. Rituals that smother our goals are bad rituals.

I want to be Peaceful and Simple
Nurturing and Loving
Seeking and Supportive
I want to be Witness
I want to be the Truth and the Light

These are Be-Attitudes. Many more are at:
http://www.gotwater.net/be_attitudes.htm

GOOD RITUALS—BAD RITUALS

Reflecting on rituals and spirituality, a ninety-year-old Friend shared his recollections about weighty Friends and recorded ministers of his youth who, for decades, filled the facing benches of this and other Quaker meetings. By virtue of their steadfast presence, they provided the spiritual backbone of the community.

I have felt, in a much shorter time span, the same spiritual presence of Friends here. Paul Brown, who sat on the bench in front of me for many years, comes to mind the most. His advanced age and lack of mobility limited our interaction to shaking hands and brief exchanges at the rise of meeting, but Paul has left a definite mark and presence.

In the context of good rituals and bad rituals, my thoughts drift to my own grandfather. My grandfather was a very learned and very religious man, who obeyed all the laws of his religion and followed all its rituals to the letter. I did not know him and, regrettably, know very little about his life.

But recently, I found a postcard his sent to his niece a few years before his death. By the time of the writing, he was a broken, dispirited man. His closing comment says it all: "We must live out this burdensome life," he wrote. My grandfather endured many hardships in his years, and it is clearly not my place to judge him.

But I must ask myself, did the laws and the rituals of his religion help or hinder? They weren't only demanding in time and money, they also dictated giving life and providing for eleven children. He must have found some sustenance and comfort in those rituals, but the fact remains: To my grandfather, life was a duty not a privilege.

WHAT'S IN FORGIVENESS?

A sappy movie brings it all together. On his deathbed, a man tells his son: "I forgave you. It changed everything." It then goes on to portray convincingly two scenarios in the man's life—one with forgiveness, the other without. And behold, forgiveness did change everything.

In the name of justice for the victim, "sin" commonly results in the punishment of the offender. But retribution does not bring peace to the victim's soul. And as justice for one may mean injustice for another, the cycle of ill will may go on forever.

Forgiveness benefits the victim more than the perpetrator. And what if the victim and the perpetrator are one and the same? When the "sinner" is no other than the self, the punishment is the worst, which is why forgiveness to oneself is more difficult than to others.

*   *

An Old Testament passage claims that the sins of the fathers carry to three and four generations. That math has always puzzled me. Was it three or four? Either way, how can that knowledge be so precise?

Hearing Jesus say "forgive your brother's sins not seven times but seventy times seven times," it dawned on me the biblical numbers were not math formulae but figures of speech. Sins of fathers carry for "many" generations.

Forgiveness goes beyond sins and bad people. Without closure and forgiveness, even minor matters can torment the souls of proverbial fathers. They will affect those who are around now and for many generations to come.

QUAKERS ARE CHRISTIANS—JESUS WAS BOTH

Quakers are the Religious Society of Friends. Informally, though, Quakers are better known as Friends. That is a fair state of affairs, for few Friends today refer to the Religious Society and especially the religious part.

Friends do have religious beliefs and testimonies result thereof. With "love your neighbor" behind them, values such as social justice and peace become self-evident.

The peace testimony, too, has deep religious roots. War is evil, and the Spirit that had led away from it is not changeable to lead back to it.

In a simplistic form, Quakerism comes down to three words: Truthful—Peaceful—Simple. That was the gist of a show presented on Community Day.

For good measure, "Follow the Teachings of Jesus" was tagged on, for too many good people know too little about Friends and ask questions as silly as: "Are Quakers Christian?"

Friends are not always inclined to discuss it, but the fact is that Quakerism has its roots in seventeenth century European Christianity. Early Quakers rebelled not against religion but against the trappings of the Church at that time.

Early Friends preferred the simple worship as it had been in the first days of the Church. Their worship was guided solely by the Inner Light. Their beliefs came from the teachings of Jesus. In fact, a close look at those teaching makes it rather clear that Jesus himself was a Quaker.

The first Quaker

AUTHORITY BY GOD AND MEN

Francis Brown was a remarkable Friend. He lent Quaker witness to the community for over half a century. He shaped our meeting in many ways, providing spiritual leadership and moral compass like no other.

Francis Brown had spiritual authority, said a Friend at his memorial service who had known him well. Through decades of leadership, Friends gain certain authority in meeting. But Francis had more.

*   *

At the Temple, the Chief Priests ask Jesus: "By what authority do you do these things?" Jesus does not answer but makes it clear that there is an authority by God that is different from authority by men.

Through His ministry, Jesus gained divine authority to advance the Kingdom of Heaven. His disciples got the authority from Jesus to do the same. That is what Jesus is telling the High Priests.

All human beings are endowed with divine authority to shine and share their God-given Inner Light. That is granted. By default, that authority supersedes all other.

*   *

Leadings of the Spirit often come in conflict with the rules of men. Whenever that happened, Francis Brown knew the priorities and how to stand behind them. He knew that God's authority always comes first.

Let more Friends be like him

TWO PATHS—ONE DESTINATION

We have visitors with us today. My sister-in-law and her family are visiting from New England. They have been Friends as long as I have, and this weekend, I have finally gotten around asking her how that happened.

It was revealing to hear that her spiritual journey has been similar to mine. She, too, had looked for the truth and had tried a number of things to help find it. She has been a seeker like me and like many of us here today.

My sister-in-law comes from a different religious background and a different upbringing than mine. Even though we travelled different paths, we have arrived at similar conclusions and came to the same place. To me, that was comforting, and as family, it has brought us closer together.

The revelation was also comforting for another reason. Sitting in worship together, I realized that we may have come from different places and may have stumbled upon different facets of the same truth, but it had been Quakerism that gave us the freedom to do so.

Quakerism today is among the religions that allow the most leeway for personal journeys and for the seeking of a personal path. "God is a personal experience" makes me think of that freedom. Rather than following dogma, Friends may find their own divine truth.

It has been said that Quakerism is as appealing for what it isn't as for what it is. The lack of binding doctrine is certainly among them. While Friends are not always at ease stating Quaker beliefs, personal experience of God is one worthy of mention.

WHAT'S IN A WORD?

A wise man once said if you kept going in one direction, you might end up where you were headed. In a lifetime of spiritual travel, we move great distances. A tiny shift in direction at the start may take us to a totally different place, making us a very different person.

I was a free-spirited teenager when an orthodox great uncle paid us a visit. He quipped about our religious differences: "It is what makes the world around." His comment got deeply imprinted in my mind. It may have been the very shift that makes Friends tolerance so appealing to me today.

Soon after that, a good friend of mine said no one person can fix all of the world's problems. That, too, stayed with me and, unlike many Friends today who want to fix the world, I try to go after one problem at a time.

People we encounter in our spiritual journey become part of us and change who we are. That is true for the meeting community and for Friends who are no longer with us. Their legacy lives on.

I am thinking in particular of Hugh, who provided the leadership to start up the Friendly Bible class. I called Hugh while he was in the hospital. He asked that we go ahead with the class without him. He died shortly after that. To me, his words weren't a request but an order.

0000Words speak to us when we need them most. Some speak to us louder than others. Perhaps it is a matter of openness and need for direction. As people become part of us, and we become part of them, *our* own words may speak the loudest when needed most.

THE LAST WILL BE FIRST

A recent cartoon is a take-off Pavlov's reflex-conditioning experiment. In this case, the dog does the talking. "Look," says the dog, "Every time I walk to my food, that guy nods his head, and writes in his book." The cartoon is funny by being absurd.

Jesus uses the parable of the vineyard to illustrate the seemingly absurd in the spiritual world. In the Kingdom of Heaven, he says "The last will be first, and the first will be last." It is a reminder that ordinary rules don't always apply as expected.

In a workshop I led, I noted that outward absurdity may not be so absurd after all. If your basket is full of apples and you give some away, you will have fewer apples. But love given from a heart full of love will bring more love to it.

In an ordinary discussion, words are heard and responded to accordingly. That is what we know, and that is what we expect. But in vocal ministry, one can never be sure who hears the words, or when and how a message may touch someone.

In a world of cause and effect, it would be absurd to keep going without results. But life by those rules alone yields heartbreak, for in matters of the Spirit, results are far from evident. In the world of the Spirit, results are in the realm of faith. Motivation is not a matter of results but a matter of doing "the right thing."

After the workshop, I noticed a giant banner
Sow the Seed—Trust the Promise

I couldn't have said it better

IF BUDDHA KNEW THE LIGHT

Few Friends today remember Lou and his rich vocal ministry.

Lou often spoke of his passion for reading the dictionary. I recall that well, for I do the same.

Dictionaries hold a treasure of wisdom about word origins and linguistic connections. Dictionaries may also present semantic surprises.

Sanctions, for example, may mean approval or denial; left may indicate departure or remainder, while continue may be an order to go on or to stop, and custom is something either standard or tailored. These are some of the so called contronyms.

They remind me of the quote: "Believe nothing—no matter where you read it or who said it—unless it agrees with your own reasoning and your own common sense."

The quote is attributed to Buddha, and if Buddha could, he would have simply said to trust your Inner Light.

The Inner Light is

More powerful than any opinion of men

The ultimate test of truth

The ultimate spiritual detector of the Divine

Friends most trusted and cherished companion

WHAT'S MINE—WHAT ISN'T?

With "Render unto Caesar that which is Caesar's and unto God that which is God's," Jesus delineates the material world and world of the Spirit. There is no need to choose one over the other, for they can coexist without imposition.

In the course of studying the passage, a Friend wondered if we could expand the separation to the personal level. What *is* mine and what *is* yours? That intriguing and unresolved query resurfaced unexpectedly.

Our daughter graduated from college with a sense of achievement and great spirit. She thanked me for all the support that had enabled her to do that. While feedback is a blessing I relish, I told her there was no need for gratitude because *she* was my reward.

It took twenty years of feeding and protection, example and guidance, nurture and inspiration. She—the end result of all that—was my success. My comment didn't go down well. Was I taking away the merits of her work?

Whose success was it; mine or hers? I did what I did because it had to be done, and I did it the only way I knew how. It was the right thing to do. Whether my daughter returns gratitude or not, in my heart, her success was mine.

*   *

I seek no recognition for doing the work of the Spirit. I am grateful for the leadings of the Spirit given to me. Success belongs to all the Friends who stand by me and share the Light. Praise belongs to the Spirit.

Jesus would likely say: Praise my Father in Heaven

BE WITH THE PRESENT—BE IN THE LIGHT

"The past is a lesson, the present is a gift." That powerful affirmation has been with me all week. Looking at the present as a precious gift—with or without the pun—forces me to examine my choices carefully each and every day.

Minding the leadings of the Spirit is the best use of a day's life. At the end of the day, I can ask: Am I happy with the choices I made? Have I done well all that I had set out to do? Can I do better another day with another gift of life?

The past is merely a lesson to learn from. I, however, struggle with the past. Even if the past cannot be changed, darkness from the past enters the mind. What if things would have been just a bit different?

I struggle with my own shortcomings the most. Even though I acted with a pure heart and in the Light of the Spirit, even though I did the best I knew how at that time, the darkness still comes to the surface.

A Friend said: "I strive to be in the Light, but at times, I find myself in darkness. Instead of trying to work my way out of the darkness, though, I ought to just stay in the Light." That message spoke directly to my condition.

The darkness is in the past

Rather than wrestling with the past
I, too, am better off staying in the Light

I shall take my gift of the present
And stay in the Light

130

TRAVELING FRIENDS

As on similar occasions in the past, Friends may wonder: Who are the strangers in the room? What brings them here? What it is they are looking for? In this case, we are not completely strangers. We are traveling Friends.

Unlike traveling Friends of John Woolman's days, we have no Friendly letter of introduction. We are not here for the sake of ministry or to preach for a cause. We have simply travelled to see our daughter, who has moved to the area.

We *are* Friends—members of Downingtown Meeting.

We do bring to you the energy of our spiritual home, rich in spiritual life and blessed with abundant vocal ministry. It is a vibrant meeting, where eighty to a hundred Friends gather on First Days to continue the flow of uninterrupted worship on every First Day since 1806.

Downingtown Meeting is in the heart of the Quaker State, and Chester County, Pennsylvania is home to the highest concentration of Quaker meetings anywhere in the world. In fact, within a radius of ten miles, there are more meetings than you can count on two hands.

We are proud heirs of William Penn's Holy Experiment, as we are proud of his twenty-seven-ton statue adorning Philadelphia's City Hall.

We feel the presence of the thousands of Friends who worshiped before us. We draw on the energy of the hundreds of Friends around us who worship and honor the Spirit in their own special way today.

That is the spiritual energy we bring you today

THE CAPTAIN AND THE TRUTH

It's been a while since a joke has been heard in worship. So here is a favorite of mine:

It's midnight. The captain is on the bridge of the ship for final inspection. He sees a bright object straight ahead. He signals right away: "You are on collision course. Move ten east; over." The response is immediate: "You are on collision course. Move ten west; over."

The captain is in no mood for games. "I am Captain Jones," he says "move ten east; over." "I am Attendant Matthews. Move ten west; over." The captain is furious. "I am a U.S. destroyer with five thousand sailors onboard," he barks; "I'm not moving!" "I am the Lighthouse with one part-time help; your choice."

Why am I telling this? Because who you are or what you say—be it the commander of a destroyer or the keeper of the lighthouse—doesn't change facts. A lighthouse will remain a lighthouse, no matter what.

For Friends, seekers of the truth, that is an important message. Truth may be mysterious and elusive. When found, it may prove to be inconvenient, controversial, and even painful.

But truth is immutable. In the search of the immutable truth, Friends must put aside who they are and what position they may hold in life. They must ignore all things they may have heard and any preconceived ideas they may have had.

In the search for truth
One thing only matters—truth itself

132

GIVE ME YOUR COAT

One day, I noticed an amazing red astilbe in my neighbor's garden. "I have never seen a thing like that," I exclaimed.

Since the best plants come from exchanges with other gardeners, I told him I wouldn't mind having a piece of it.

My neighbor obliged. He dug it up the whole plant and gave it to me. That seemed a bit strange.

Being afraid he might take his whole house apart, I didn't ask him for anything else after that.

*   *

Equally strange and enigmatic is the verse from Matthew: "If a stranger wants your coat, give him your tunic too." I have had trouble digesting that—spiritually or otherwise. Perhaps others do too.

But the verse in Matthew's may not be about money or sacrifice but about recognizing and honoring the Spirit of the fellow man. My neighbor understood that.

At that point in time, a red astilbe did more for me than it did for him. His motivation as well as Matthew's passage began to make sense.

*   *

This week, I found a rare red astilbe in the store. I bought it and placed it on my neighbor's porch. I am waiting to see what happens next.

A JOYFUL SONG TO THE LORD

Our year-end Friendly Bible class was a joyful song.

Shout for joy to the LORD all land
Worship the LORD with gladness
Come before Him with joyful song
God is who made us
We are His people the sheep of His pasture
Enter His gates with thanksgiving and His courts with praise
The LORD is good and His love endures forever

I could not rejoice with the others and felt bad for bringing the mood down. My aversion to the Old Testament was born long before I become a Friend, and even in this love-filled verse, I sensed partiality. The verse belongs to His people and is sung by His people.

While the Kingdom taught by Jesus is a world for all to prosper and to live in peace, the Old Testament is a zero-sum game, where well-being comes at the expense of others. Simply, the Old Testament is a covenant of an exclusive God who crushes the enemies of His "chosen" people.

George Fox bolsters the peace testimony by espousing a life that eliminates all reason for war. Life championed in the Old Testament makes war not only inevitable but advisable. God whose divine orders must be obeyed, commands the most barbaric retribution for historical events which the subjects have nothing to do with.

Thou shalt blot out the remembrance of Amalec from under Heaven
Go and strike Amalec and destroy all that they have
Kill man and woman, and infant, ox and sheep, camel and donkey

"God Bless America," too, suggests an exclusive covenant. In contrast, Friends eloquent bumper-sticker blesses the whole world—no exceptions. That includes our enemies, so they too may see the Light and the wisdom of the Kingdom.

134

THE BRANCH OF A MIMOSA

The mimosa seed I had planted grew two inches the first year, two feet in the second, and an amazing eight feet in the third. I fed it, protected it from high winds, and directed its growth to form a strong majestic canopy. At ten feet, though, things were out of my reach and out of my hands. The mimosa grew new branches, charting its own way as it was meant to do.

From afar, I watched with admiration the delicate cotton candy flowers. Without them, summers wouldn't be the same. This weekend, its longest branch bent down as if to greet me, once again within my reach. Any other time, I wouldn't have given it a second thought, except today my daughter came for an extensive visit.

Over the years, I fed her too, protected her, and steered her toward the right choices. She is now a fine young woman, mother and wife, and no one could ask for a more awesome bloom than our four-year-old granddaughter.

From afar, I have looked on with a touch of sadness as her life has taken its inevitable course. Things were out of my hands and somewhat out of my reach as well.

This weekend, though, she came. Perhaps she missed me too. We mused about old stories and told new ones. We walked, chatted, and solved puzzles. We did all the things that we have always done best.

Human ties are indelible, regardless of time or distance. I know that for sure. Still, reaffirming ours felt refreshing. In a sense, her visit was therapeutic. Suddenly, a mundane case of a low-lying mimosa branch assumed a whole new meaning.

LET THEM PRAISE YOUR FATHER IN HEAVEN

"Let your Light shine before others so they may see your good works and give praise to your Father in Heaven" is one of my favorite verses. It may best illustrate Friends as channels of the Spirit—willing implements to carry out its leadings. Praise and gratitude, therefore, are due to the Spirit that has planted seed.

Glorifying a personified universal force is practical and intuitive. But I have trouble seeing an old man with a white beard—the tyrannical, implacable, and vengeful Old-Testament God of Michelangelo—either as a source of inspiration or object of praise.

To me, God is much, much older. With Santa Claus's chubby cheeks and the satisfied smile of Buddha, God sits motionlessly on His heavenly throne in regal garb.

God was pleased with His Creation. Day after day, He stopped to review His miracles. What He had done was "good." After six days, God was done. There is nothing in Genesis about God going back to work the next Monday.

I have no problem with a personified God who created a masterpiece of perfection and is now high above on the supreme throne reveling in His Creation. I have no problem seeing that God sending His angels to guide us with leadings of the Spirit and continuing revelation.

I can see a very old God, with very white hair and a much longer beard, sitting on a very high throne surrounded by a millions packets of gratitude, like shiny presents piled under a Christmas tree.

I have no problem giving praise to a God like that

IN THE MORNING LIGHT

The best time for a walk is at the crack of dawn, before smoking cars emerge from hidden garages and before the school buses start crisscrossing the neighborhood. At times, I run into my neighbor Nick walking the miniature mutt he found on the internet, but otherwise there is no one else in sight.

It is quiet, and I am out there alone with my thoughts. I amuse myself thinking about the people in their homes preparing for their important day; men messing with shaving cream and neckties, women agonizing over the ideal outfit for their day, and desperate mothers trying to get their kids out of bed and ready for school.

This week, something was different. One morning, as I looked up ahead of me, I noticed a giant hawk sitting on the tip of the tallest tree on the hill. The first rays of light illuminated its powerful chest. I kept walking. The hawk kept sitting. The hawk was too serene to be hungry, too majestic to even think of food.

Why would a lonely bird be sitting on the top of a tree all by itself? Maybe it was depressed. I chuckled; too much people talk. Ah, I thought, it was having a meeting for worship. I chuckled again; too much Quaker talk. But the fact remained. There was a giant hawk sitting on top of that tree—to a casual eye, doing nothing.

Yet the hawk did the best thing anyone could have done on a crisp morning of fall. It reveled in the glorious new day that was about to unfold. With majesty and power, it bore active witness to the rising web of life around it. One lonely bird on top of a tree made my day. Its message was loud and clear. Just be, for being is plenty.

JOHNNY MY BEST FRIEND

Growing up, Johnny was my best friend. He was also the strongest kid around and eager to prove it in school, in the neighborhood, and…to me. In frustration, Mother said one day that if I ate my dinner I would be stronger than Johnny. I had waited years for that. I quickly gulped down the food in front of me and ran over to beat him up.

In a sad twist of events, an amused Johnny all but choked me to death instead. But I learned two things that day: not to listen to Mother and not to eat my dinner. My most valuable lesson—the one that stayed with me forever—was just how impressionable children can be. As a parent, I kept that in mind at all times.

*   *

Whenever I could, I reiterated to my children Friends motto that God is in everyone. It wasn't only to learn respect for others but learn respect for themselves, because that of God makes them as good and great as anyone else, regardless of their age or size.

Meeting brings a new dimension to that nurture. When we speak of our children, we speak of all the children of meeting. We must collectively nurture the God within them. We must teach them their undeniable self-worth and the sacredness of their Inner Light. We have the means and the opportunity to do that.

From us, they must learn to shine it in the world and that no one ever has the right to dim it or trample it over.

I shall thus ask as a query

What do we do to bolster the Spirit of our children?

138

MESSENGERS AT MY DOOR

It occurred to me just a few days ago that it has been a while since I last talked to Jehovah's Witnesses.

As if it were a sign of things to come, two young ladies showed up at my doorstep. I welcomed them and let them know it was always my pleasure to talk to them.

This time, I did most of the talking. I told them I was a Quaker. I told them about the Friendly Bible Study and about our attempt to apply the teachings of Jesus to our daily lives. I told them about the peace testimony and about George Fox's ideal to live in a world that takes away all reason for war.

It is not fair, I said, to expect some Superman to come and fix everything that we have messed up. But Jesus says we *can* all live in peace in abundance if we work together.

He showed us the way and, for that, he may be called the Messiah. But it is up to us to take the steps and bring forth the mending.

In the grand scheme of things, I said, we were on the same team, aiming for the same goals. If Friends, and Witnesses, and all others would set their idiosyncrasies aside and focus on the Kingdom of Heaven, we could all work together and achieve it. That is the Good News about the Kingdom.

To my surprise, they agreed. "That's why we go from door to door," they said.

I had no answer to that

How do *Friends* teach the Good News?

139

A MESSAGE FROM NANTUCKET

Lucretia Mott was a Nantucket Friend and women's rights advocate. I went to Nantucket this summer, not to look for her, but to find a place with a quiet beach and few quaint shops. Instead, I found a gem laden with Quaker history and full of surprises.

Without doubt, whaling had been at the core of Nantucket and its Quaker life. The bay of Nantucket was perfect for it. Once the Quakers got the idea, Nantucket whalers were crisscrossing the oceans in no time. Upon return, they brought with them the latest from the world, making Nantucket the most cosmopolitan town in America.

At the time of William Penn's nascent colony in Pennsylvania, Nantucket was a blossoming Quaker universe. Its meeting house had an incredible two thousand seats. No one could do a thing on the island without being a Quaker.

While other colonists were busy oppressing their natives and dragging slaves to their colonies, Nantucket Quakers employed not only Indians but also Africans who then came to America of their own volition. Frederick Douglass delivered his first speech in a Nantucket meeting house. Nantucket saw the first black whaling captain in history.

Whaling meant oil, and oil meant light in mills after sundown. Oil was a game changer for the early industrial revolution. But whaling meant big investment in capital and labor. How could a small island carry out such an enterprise? The answer lies in whaling bonds and end-of-trip profit-sharing. They all hinged on Quaker honesty. Without it, there would have been no whaling on Nantucket.

At its height, whaling brought in fifty thousand kills a year. The whales, though, had the last laugh. In 1846, a fire in a hat store ignited the whale oil storage on the wharf and burned down the town. It was not only an omen but the beginning of the end, for oil discovered in Pennsylvania brought an era to its end.

Nantucket is a two-century Quaker laboratory. It started with John Richardson, a Quaker preacher from England.

"Unlike the Puritans, Richardson talked not about sin and punishment but common-sense words against hatred, greed, and envy. If all followed, he said, the world would be a paradise, the Kingdom of Heaven on Earth. An hour passed. People realized these were words of Jesus. Many were sobbing. All settlers were caught up in the words of the Quaker." They all became Quakers.

It all went downhill from there. Old fractures gave birth to new ones, and Friends, while tolerant toward others, saved no effort to disown each other. They simply forgot the preacher's words. Many calamities disrupted Quaker life in Nantucket. But when the last Quaker died in 1900, thousands of others were living on the island—many disowned Quakers among them.

Working together brings paradise to Earth, Richardson said. Nantucket Friends had it for a while, but driven by pettiness, they lost sight of it. And losing sight of Paradise is the first step to losing Paradise altogether.

The message is clear. It has been my daily reminder of how good my life is and has been.

In our personal lives as in our communal life
the caveat of Nantucket is valid today as ever

WHO IS THE MESSIAH?

Our Friendly Bible Study is in its fourth year. In this week's reading, Jesus who invariably refers to himself as the Son of Man, speaks of the Messiah for the first time. There are also "rabbis," "teachers," and "folks on the seat of Moses" in that confusing passage.

The discernment of who-was-what ended when a Friend suggested that the Messiah is…us. We are the Messiah—all of us. It was a radical and far-reaching idea. The more I thought of it, though, the more sense it made and the more I liked it.

*   *

Jesus explains the spiritual nature of resurrection: "When the dead rise, they will neither marry nor be given in marriage. They will be like the angels in Heaven." In that vein, the patriarchs are also alive, for "The God of Abraham, Isaac, and Jacob is the God of the living not the God of the dead. To Him, they are all alive."

They are alive, for their Spirit lives in us. They are alive because we, in one form or another, perpetuate their Spirits. They are us. Without us, they would be dead.

Jesus and his Messianic message are alive in the same manner. Jesus has shown the ways of the Messiah to mend the world. He conferred upon all the powers of the Messiah to be workers of the Kingdom. Thus the Spirit of Messiah is alive in all of mankind. That is awesome.

Is it safe to say that the end-of-time prophecies are a thing of the past? If they have already taken place, we now have the power and the charter to mend the world ourselves.

THOSE TWO CENTS OF OURS

On this bright crisp day, rays of sunshine pour into the meeting house, engulfing the facing benches.

As a Friend fidgets in his seat, his hands change positions ever so slightly. Unbeknown to him, the light bounces off his ring and hits me every few minutes with bursts of powerful beams diffused into millions of sparkles.

They resurface a dilemma for ages on my mind. Man had seen that light forever but made no laser beams from it. He had been around electricity forever but made no use of it in his life. The elements of the Earth surrounding him forever did not give birth to advanced technology.

Modern knowledge, I believe, only came into being by the large-scale exchange among people. Even today, there isn't a single man on Earth who knows how to make a plain pencil.

The pencil factory manager doesn't know. There are people who know how to grow trees and age wood; others know where to find graphite, and others yet who make the machines to bond them together.

In that sense, scientific progress is not unlike the process in a spiritual community. Friends may worship in solitude or in nature and gain personal revelation that enriches their Spirit.

But personal revelation pales in comparison to the enlightenment a corporate body brings. As in science, breakthroughs in spiritual journeys are likely to take place only in the midst of a rich and nurturing spiritual community.

THERE IS NO OTHER

Gluttony, Wrath, and Sloth are odd words we rarely use today. They are among the seven deadly sins, the medieval construct meant to impose desirable codes of conduct. As with other ancient matters, we are likely to dismiss them as irrelevant, archaic, or simply inane.

Lust tops the list of the seven. It isn't the modern-day tabloid lust but the yearning for another place and another time; a lust for a life other than our own. It is the sin of not living in the present. That twist makes the medieval caveat expressly fit today. Lust is about boredom and the greener grass on the other side. Lust is the sin of "other."

In the course of a lively and entertaining chat with my five-year-old daughter, I, too, lapsed into a mini "other" moment. I fantasized about the day she will be an adult and the fun of our future talks. When I told her I couldn't wait for her to grow up, she snapped back: "What, you want to get rid of me?" I certainly didn't.

The cycle of life has come full circle. My five-year-old granddaughter is sweet and smart as any other kid her age. Their infinite energy is devoted to wiping out yours. Their needs bear no delay; yours mean nothing. They drag you down with tedium and repetition. Your life has been put on hold.

I sense the drain on her mother—the subject of the incessant drudgery. I sense the wish for the day be over, the wish for her sweetheart to be grown up, the wish to move on with her own life; I sense the lust for other.

But this *is* your life, I tell her. Having been on both ends, I am qualified to give advice: This *is* the best part thereof.

THE SPIRIT TOLD ME

There has never been a motivator as potent as hunger. "I am hungry" must be the most common phrase in human history.

Among thousands of other languages, Modern English may be alone to offer a special refinement: "I am hungry for." It may be a cultural reflection of choice in a world of incredible plenty. Ironically, it also points to a very important fact.

Our bodies are capable of telling us what to eat. I had known that long before I became a Friend. Then, it meant nothing. Now, it is a message from the Inner Teacher—the Inner Light. Friends may frown upon knocking the Inner Light down to such pedestrian level as food.

But in my view, the Inner Light has no limits. Its voice is confined neither to the ethereal matters of the Spirit nor to choosing the next meal.

Embodied inside each and every one of us is the script of God's Creation. Deep down in the cells, resides the wisdom of the whole Universe, more complex than we could ever imagine.

As I center and ask to heal my body, I listen openly. The answers are already there. The Inner Light has them. They have been inside for a very long time. They are worthier than expert opinions and more relevant than book-learned medical standards.

If Creation is God's Creation, and if we cannot grasp the complexity of God, all we can do is expect guidance into the right direction. All *I* can do is ask and listen.

TOTAL SURRENDER

A man was put in a situation he resented. Total surrender was the only way out, but still, he resisted his predicament strenuously. We are conditioned to be autonomous, to pursue goals, to do what is right, to take a stand. Total surrender is not a natural condition of every-day life.

Once the man did surrender, he actually liked what happened and was reluctant to leave. The man's adventure was only a dream, but total surrender left its mark on me.

In our spiritual lives, we seek the voice of the Divine and the leadings of the Spirit. We do want to heed the voice, and we do want to follow the leading. Why then is total spiritual surrender a struggle?

My struggle has been mostly in worship. It starts with the stir of a thought. I become restless. I feel the pull of the Spirit in the room. Grudgingly, I hunt for words. More thoughts evolve. I must put them in logical order. I feel the compelling force to share. What is the message?

Over and over, I blaze through the discerning circle. It's all there. The last step is permission of the Spirit to speak. Seemingly, I have it, but I resist. I am torn. Gone is the calmness of heart. Resistance flies in the face of worship. It must end. At once!

Total surrender is a powerful concept. By now, it has gotten my full attention. Total surrender means honoring the Spirit. Total surrender means acceptance.

*   *

The supreme acceptance is the acceptance of missteps:
Failings of others—but mostly of mine

146

A WORSHIPFUL PLACE

Hanazono shrine is a stone throw away from the busiest train station in the world. It is an oasis in the midst of the mad hustle, a tranquil place of prayer before a day's work. Like Japan's other ninety thousand shrines, it is an emblem of the sacred in life much as a Quaker meeting is.

I love visiting meetings, be it around us or in my travels to other states. The faces of Friends become faint, and their messages get lost in time. But with each visit a bright spot appears on the imaginary map I carry in my mind. It casts a beacon of truth, love, and goodwill far and wide from its tiny equivalent on an ordinary map.

I feel the spiritual power of that oasis as I approach the first traffic light on my way to *our* meeting. I hope our visiting Friends today will depart taking that power with them. Not everyone can feel it, I am sure. A first-time visitor to Friends worship is likely to wonder about the strange folk seated in silence in a plain room.

A first-time visitor is not likely to recognize that of all the places those folks could have been, they chose to come and gather here in worship. By sitting in silent expectation as a corporate body, they create the sacred place for that worship—the most important thing they do.

I reflect on this today as my visiting daughter, who after a long absence, is once again sitting by my side. She may tell her friends that she came to meeting with me. "What did you do there?" they may ask. "Nothing." "What did you talk about?" "Nothing." "Were you *mad* at each other…?"

Yet, sitting in meeting together is the highlight of her visit for both of us. It's hard to explain, let alone understand.

A PLACE WE CALL HOME

"Daddy," said an old note in the drawer, "With so much water on Earth, is there a chance that we will drink the same water twice?"

It was a question once posed by my eight-year-old daughter. It gave me a chuckle and some food for thought. After all, stewardship queries come in all different shapes and forms.

It took a transatlantic flight and the enormity of the ocean below to gain a sense of just how much water there was on Earth. Plus, I got a sense of the hard-to-grasp magnitude of the Earth itself. That Earth, on which people tread as invisible ants, seemingly immune to such petty disruption, is a tender system in a delicate balance.

That balance has been achieved by billions of years of iterative adjustments. They have resulted in a precisely-tuned body of air and water, light and heat, suitable for human life—a planet we call home. The Earth's surface cooled off, its air came into being, poisons were buried in great depths, and edible food became sufficient.

A large colony of ants is able to alter the landscape, but a storm or two can easily restore it. It may take eons to mend the aftermath of man's actions on Earth, even if they prove to be reversible. It is evident that people on Earth today are no longer just petty irritants but a danger to Earth itself.

The mix of cosmic conditions that enabled life on Earth as we know it may not exist anywhere else in the Universe.

Earth is our only home, and yet
We treat it as if we had another one to go to

A DAY ON THE SQUARE

Kennett Friends Meeting is a two story stone building in Kennett Square, PA. and home to a recent gathering of Friends. Our spacious meeting room on the upper floor was filled with an air of welcome and tons of light. It snowed throughout the day, and as Friends sat in closing worship, big lazy flakes still came down in great numbers.

They were a metaphor for the many concerns Friends had brought with them. Friends wrestled with hefty matters, some of which eluded imminent solution. They weighed Friends down and sapped the spiritual energy of their home meetings. Just how many of them found resolution that day is, of course, hard to tell but one thing was quite clear.

No matter how many snowflakes came down, no matter how big they were, none of them touched us. They all went by the wayside. We could see them; they could see us. But they couldn't touch us.

No matter how many flakes came down or for how long, it would have taken years of steady snowfall to reach us in the spirit-filled room. Moreover, by then, some of the older ones would have melted without hurting a soul.

That serene, metaphoric scene was a precious take-away.

It was Friends powerful reminder to be in the Light, to dwell in unity *above* conflicting matters, and to work around them. Let them go by the wayside and melt away.

As the snow in Kennett's spirit-bound meeting room, those concerns, no matter how indomitable on the surface, are powerless in face of the Spirit. They are able to inflict only a momentary if pleasant distraction.

QUAKERS ARE FRIENDS

Some years ago a T-shirt came out. "Quakers are Friends," it proclaimed. I liked that shirt a lot. "Quakers" is dark and foreboding, but "Friends" is lighter, timelier, and more hip. It is a bit amusing too, for hearing "Friends," I can't help thinking of sandboxes full of kids.

Pendle Hill pamphlet *Beyond Consensus* raises a question I have never thought of asking: Whose friends are Friends or friends of what? Are they friends of everybody or just friends of themselves? Are they friends of peace and the environment or friends of the downtrodden?

Friends have always been champions of peace and justice, and they have been friends of each other in times of need. But above all, early Friends were friends of the truth, the pamphlet says, and their Religious Society was the Society of Friends of the Truth.

The unwavering search for truth is indeed the noblest of virtues. But that can be good news or bad news. To Friends today who romanticize the days of George Fox, it is bad news, for early Friends were as rigid and intolerant in their truth as those whom they were shunning.

Over the years, Friends have shown that no unity of Spirit can overcome intolerance. That is not a good thing to romanticize about. Two centuries too late, unity did prevail. Had it happened when it mattered most, there could be millions of Friends in this country today.

Rigidity is now gone, but unwavering search for truth is not. Today, Friends may seek the truth in their own particular way, and that is a truly invaluable gift to Friends. I wouldn't have it any other way.

150

SPIRIT-LED ELDERING

For good reasons, perhaps, a particular worship meeting would not settle. At last, a weighty Friend spoke: "Two skeletons hung in the closet. One skeleton said to the other: 'If I had any guts I'd get out of here.'" Meeting soon settled. The ancient vignette shows the power of humor in eldering.

Historically, eldering was applied to enforce discipline as outlined in the Books of Discipline of yearly meetings—the discipline of towing the official line in effect at that time. This anecdote brings to mind *Spirit-led Eldering,* the exciting Pendle Hill pamphlet recently read in the Friendly Book Club.

The pamphlet presents a new and transformative aspect of eldering. In contrast to discipline-rooted admonishment, spirit-led eldering opens the door to spiritual leadership. Its objective is not only to support the spiritual life of the individual but also that of the community.

Spirit-led eldering spans mentoring connections and social events, where Friends insights may be shared. Worship, Care and Counsel, and Clearness Committees are all sources of spiritual nurture. Nominating Committees are suited to unearth the gifts of new Friends and assist in finding their right-ordered place in meeting.

Spirit-led eldering demands preparedness. It rests on seasoned, well-grounded divine intention. Spirit-led eldering requires time to explore the condition of the elderee. Spirit-led eldering cannot be impulsive or reactive.

The result of spirit-led eldering is not only nurture but broad affirmation and restoration.

A THOUSAND POINTS OF LIGHT

Hundreds of miles from here, there is a centuries-old stone building. Extra-large windows on three sides bring in sunlight throughout most of the day. Its one room is lined with ancient wooden benches facing in one direction. Seated on them in worship, at this very moment, are a hundred or so Friends; the same exact way as we are here now.

Most Friends sit on the same spot week after week. I can see them in great detail. One Friend has sat on the same facing bench for nearly four decades. His large earlobes light up as the rays of light shoot through the windows at the right angle. It's a regular event, a signal perhaps that meeting has settled.

The Spirit is strong. A Friend may be delivering a message at this very instant. Hardly a week goes by without a handful of Friends doing so. The carvings in the wooden benches attest to generations of others who spent a lifetime in worship there. It is our home meeting. Around it, there are dozens others with hundreds of other worshipping Friends.

There are thousands more Friends across the country doing the same—thousands more points of real Light. It is a powerful spiritual statement. Whether I sit here or in my home meeting, the image of all those bright spots blanketing the country gives me a feeling of comfort.

To me, visiting new meetings, meeting of new Friends, and experiencing their unique communal spirit is a cherished Quaker gift. Everywhere I go, I feel at ease and welcome. Everywhere I go, every meeting I attend feels as if I were at home—a home away from home.

WAS JESUS A CHRISITAN?

Last week's Friendly Bible class was about the High Priest in Jerusalem probing if Jesus was the Son of God. I was miffed. The "Son of God" was a Roman construct. How would the Jewish High Priest even know about that?

I was still reeling from my confusion when a news clip came on: "Jesus wasn't a Christian." Great! Christianity is about Jesus, and he is not a Christian?

A "Christian" film came to the rescue. A young woman becomes unexpectedly pregnant. The world caves in around her. She is fired from her high-profile job, her partner evaporates, and her sanctimonious Christian family disowns her. She is left in the dark, facing a life-decision with no financial or spiritual support.

Redemption comes from a beautician—a devout Christian herself—who senses the woman's woe and offers help. She lends a hand in small matters, but above all, she restores the young woman's Spirit. Soon, the young woman stands firmly on her feet and becomes able to minister to others.

Side by side, I saw two very different kinds of Christians. Her family, focused on sin, crucifixion, and the divinity of Jesus, abandons their daughter in her darkest hour. In that sense, Jesus wasn't a Christian, for Jesus teaches the exact opposite: Help those who need it the most.

Jesus teaches about the power of the Spirit. He believes in empathy and social justice. His Kingdom of Heaven is a world where all people work together and live in harmony—the epitome of Friends testimonies. Maybe the news clip was right. Jesus wasn't a Christian. He was a Quaker. The first Quaker.

FROM VILLAIN TO BENEFACTOR

Conflict resolution is Friends most talked-about theme. To me, the best conflict resolution is the one that addresses the roots of the conflict and eliminates them *before* conflict takes shape.

Protracted conflict ends in confrontation. The end result of that, in various forms, are a villain and a victim. Most often, the post-conflict discourse takes place from the vantage of the victim. How does the victim handle the loss and the pain? Will the victim forgive the perpetrator and under what circumstances?

A young woman's story shifted my focus. Her spiritual emptiness leads her to behaviors hurtful not only to her but to everyone around her. Her best friend becomes a bitter casualty. With transformation, the woman realizes, better than anyone, the grave impact of her actions.

She accepts her social ostracism and tries to make amends unilaterally. When the victimized ex-friend encounters dire financial impasse, she readily offers help.

Recognizing genuine transformation, her friend accepts the olive branch. She sees that her enemy became her friend. Two new aspects have crystalized for me.

The first is about the villain. In the wake of a hurtful clash, the villain faces mental angst as severe as the victim. The villain has much healing to do as well.

The second is about the conflict. For a conflict to be truly resolved, the past villain must not only become a benefactor, but more importantly, must be perceived as one.

IN THE PRESENCE OF THE DIVINE

Friends worship in "silent expectation" in the presence of the Divine. The essence of Quaker worship is the clearing of our minds and heart to hear God's voice and to receive His presence.

In my home meeting, silent worship rarely happens. As I sit here in this large and welcoming room, however, I listen intently to the silence in an attempt to feel that presence.

The notion of being in the divine presence has a wide range of interpretations. J. Doyle Penrose's ubiquitous *The Presence in the Midst* comes to mind. Friends are immersed in deep worship, and God stands solemnly by the facing benches.

It is a depiction of early Quakers, no doubt, for I know no Friends who can relate to that today. It certainly doesn't speak to my own condition.

My favorite quote also came to the surface. "Wherever you go, no matter what the weather is, always bring your own sunshine with you." Be it in worship or elsewhere we may go, we always bring with us that of God within us.

In worship, therefore, our collective presence and our divine selves form a sacred space and a manifestation of the Divine. That is the core and foundation of corporate worship.

I relish reasoning that makes sense whichever way you turn it and speaks to whomever chooses to deliberate it.

That kind of divine presence is fairly evident

155

NO GOFER TO GOD

"What do Quakers do?" asks the seeker. "It's a bit hard to explain," answers the Friend. "Well, what do Quakers believe in?" the seeker continues. "I can't really tell you for we don't have creeds," the Friend replies. "You don't have creeds?" the seeker exclaims, not even a teeny-tiny creed?" "We don't believe in creeds," concludes the Friend.

Even without creeds or beliefs, Friends do believe in their ability to have a direct channel to God. In fact, a recent QuakerSpeak video presents that ability as raison d'être for being a Quaker and as the main point of attraction to would-be seekers from the outside.

But direct access to God is merely a carryover from George Fox's battle cry against the State Church in his time. To early Friends that meant opposition to Church hirelings to run their spiritual affairs. Friends did maintain a hierarchy of elders, recorded ministers, and weighty Friends who preached lengthy sermons about Jesus and the Inner Light.

Modern Friends did away with virtually all structure. Without a defined structure and without visible ceremony, the spiritual core of modern-day Quakerism becomes more nebulous, more difficult to discern, and increasingly harder to explain. Yet Friends tend to see worship in silence sufficient for spiritual transformation.

Accordingly, anyone who comes to a meeting or two is able to absorb in silence everything there is in Quakerism and be miraculously transformed. To me, the notion that a person can walk into a meeting and soak up from thin air the spirit of worship, or the essence of Friends spiritual life, or concepts as continuing revelation and the Inner Light, is simply absurd.

156

WHY BE A QUAKER?

If George Fox had Facebook, Friends today would not be Friends. Why? Facebook already took "friends." Facebook also has a group of six thousand Friend friends from all corners of the world. It's a round-the-clock meeting for worship. Friends can share their leadings and wisdom and, via "likes," see if their message speaks to the condition of others.

Preparing for a retreat, a Facebook Friend started a jocular top-ten list of reasons for being a Quaker. Lack of snake handling and a legit belief in dinosaurs were the first two. I offered my two cents relating to the efficiency of business meetings and Jim Nayler's refusal to kiss Fox's foot.

Joking aside, I asked myself what were the top real reasons for being a Quaker. So I started my own list: Quakerism has reaffirmed my core values. continuing revelation gives purpose and meaning to my life. Others chimed in with the Inner Light and the growth of the Spirit.

In the end, humor won over essence five to one. Ironically, my favorite line came from a Friend who, by his own admission, wasn't a Friend or even an attender but an exploring seeker. "I want to be a Quaker for the promptings of truth and love in Friends hearts," he said.

Are Friends really that much into humor, I wondered? Perhaps we are just tired of talking about serious stuff. That may be part of the reason. But is it also possible that we don't talk much about Quakerism because we don't know how to?

Do we lack the words to tell the world
why we keep doing what we all keep doing?

ON QUAKER EXCITEMENT

A short while ago, I took part in a called meeting. Eighty or so Friends attended. For starters, we formed a circle and took turns sharing a good thing about our meetings. After an hour of sharing plus an hour of worship, Friends were in a somber cloud. And so, by the time my turn came, I had nothing to share.

I just stood up and asked: Are we excited to be Quakers? I felt a stir in the room. "Who is this guy?" "What is he saying?" As the stir ebbed, a Friend quipped: "This is what Quakers look like when they are excited." There was nothing to add, but I couldn't help asking myself, "What happens when they aren't?"

Excitement has many shades; thrill, passion, elation, joy, animation, to name a few. Of all the variations, I like ebullience the best. Ebullience means boiling over, and boiling over with excitement is when you are simply beyond yourself. I, for one, have been obsessing with Quaker excitement ever since the gathering.

What happens when you read a good book or see a great movie? What happens when your kid does something totally outrageous? You grab the first person who listens and talk your head off. Friends *can* be excited.

I am excited about Quakerism, and I do want to talk about it. In fact, I'd like to see ALL Friends be excited about it. I'd like to see a new movement of Quaker Excitement.

Something big. Something ambitious like a wave. A global wave with a catchy name sounding like Quaker Quest or Quaker Speak. Maybe…Quaker Kindle, although that may already be taken.

Rachel Ernst Stahlhut is excited about what Quakerism has to offer. I share her excitement because she hit the nail on the head. Quakerism has a lot to offer, to many people. But Quakerism can also offer something that no one else can. The way Callid Keefe-Perry puts it speaks to me the best.

His "Spiritual Formation" label captures the heart and soul of Quakerism. Quakerism offers a spiritual oasis—a safe harbor—where with guidance and nurture, but more importantly, without the yoke of intolerable dogma, one can look inward and discern the kind of person they are called to be and what they are called to do with their lives.

Quakerism is for everyone, Rachel says, because the Light is, and has always been in the heart of every man. Friends have been champions of that Light like no others.

I *am* excited to be a Quaker and so, I must say
I am excited to be a Quaker for the

10-Affirmation of my core values:
Peaceful—Truthful—Simple
9-Gift of the Inner Light
8-Gift of God's way to relate to others
7-Call to grow my spiritual Life
6- Purpose and inspiration through continuing revelation
5-Gift to the path of a family spiritual life
4-Opening to spiritual formation
3-Freedom to follow my own spiritual path
2-Gift of unburdened spirituality
Above all
I am excited to be a Quaker for the promptings of
truth and love in Friends hearts

The wave of Quaker Excitement is an ambitious vision
Are Friends moved to make it happen?

159

MEETING FOR WORSHIP IS LIKE...

Jesus teaches about the Kingdom of Heaven, but he never says what the Kingdom is. It is simply too hard to explain. Instead, Jesus compares the Kingdom to familiar things that people might understand. Is the Kingdom harder to explain than meeting for worship? I don't know. But I, too, like to make simple comparisons.

I once said that meeting for worship was like a spiritual beehive. Perhaps meeting for worship is like going to the movies. The room and the viewers may be the same, but the movie changes from week to week. Extended silence in a theater draws hoots and jeers, but here it invites our homemade movie to start.

I couldn't have spoken this message a decade ago, but don't laugh! While nine million people went to the premier of X-Men—the year's biggest hit—over one hundred million go onto Facebook, every day, to relish their own self-made creations.

Friends come back, week after week, for a home-spun movie. We don't know what it will be, only that it will be good. How good depends on what we bring to it. It can be very good if we come prepared and in the Spirit; if we are fired up by continuing revelation or simply excited to be gathered in the Light.

Jesus did not say what the Kingdom was. Perhaps he avoided the matter by design, to leave latitude for the future. Likewise, meeting for worship has changed quite a bit over the centuries, and to quote Francis Brown:

It is upon us to redefine it anew in each generation

AROUND AND AROUND THE SUN

Friends are like the planets around the sun, says Arthur Larrabee, different in size, and orbiting at different speeds. But they are tied to the sun by a single force—gravity. In Arthur's metaphor, that force is Friends belief system.

"A well-defined set of beliefs is vital to the viability of Friends. Thus, describing the sun is more important than describing the planets."

Quakerism, however, is not a Newtonian module of gravity but a living organism nurtured by the energy at its center— the light and warmth of the above said sun. Without the sun's nurturing energy, there would be no life, let alone Quakers on this planet.

The Inner Light *is* our core belief—the common source that binds us as Friends.

The Inner Light will always be there, emanating spiritual energy and a continuous flow of revelation, with or without a description of the out-of-reach sun. Without it, though, Quakerism will die, for unlike the gravity-confined planets, no one is tethered to it. Without nurture, Friends and seekers will simply drift away.

As such, should Friends order of the day be the sun or the planets? Gravity or the Light? Beliefs or nurture?

The sun is out of reach, but we *are* quite capable of describing ourselves. Sharing our personal adventures with the Light and the ways we are moved by them is the much needed vital nurture to enrich Friends and seekers alike.

CURLY MEANT THE INNER LIGHT

My neighbor and I exchanged pleasantries for twenty years but never really talked. At last, yielding to my many invites, he paid me a visit. "You look well," I said in jest, "compared to me, you are a young man." "Far from it," he quipped, "But my trust in the Creator gives me a worry-free life." It was the best rendition for "life-force" of his Vietnamese culture.

His comment reminded me of Curly—*City Slickers'* ultimate cowboy. Sitting by the campfire under the desert stars, Mitch—the worry-filled city slicker—poses the big question. "What is the secret of life, Curly?" Curly raises a hand with an extended index finger. "Your finger?" chuckles Mitch. "It's one," Curly smiles. "You pick what it is, but that's it. It's only one."

It was Curly's lesson in choices and priorities. There must be a source—one and only—a wellspring of vigor and strength. Curly's finger clinched it for Mitch. For my neighbor, the choice was a unique way to the "Creator." Many cultures recognize the inner life-force. In China it is called Qi; in India Kundalini. Friends call it the Light.

The Light is a life-force, in place since the day we were born. The hymn about George Fox claims the Light was there when the world began. The Light is not conditional or negotiable. To me, the Light is a source of joy and empowerment. The connection to and the awareness of the Light brings me excitement and endless possibilities.

As the old Quaker saying goes, the Light is in there, inside everyone. You just need to get it out. Thank you, my neighbor, for the timely reminder!

162

CAN'T LEGISLATE MEETING

Forty-five-year-old Beth was a very intelligent and very successful but very unhappy woman. In trying to salvage a promising love relationship, she laments her personal reserve. That reserve, she believes, was the result of growing up with parents, who had never expressed feelings to one another. She had assumed that was normal. The parents' example became the norm.

In the meeting community, we often consider the influence we have on other Friends, either through vocal ministry, spiritual nurture, or simply by ongoing personal interaction. We rarely think of our actions and deeds as standards setters. For better or worse, however, our collective practices in meeting not only set the norm, but certain customs become normal.

Just after Labor Day, I spent a quiet night at an airport hotel. The next morning, however, I was hit by a tsunami of travelers munching on free breakfast in the tight lobby. I escaped through the front door unharmed. The clusters of smokers outside brought Beth to mind and the fact that not too long ago, the shoe had been on the other foot.

Not too long ago, the mass of people inside that tight lobby would have been the smokers and the cluster outside those who escaped the living hell. I still marvel how, virtually overnight, all public places around us became smoke free. But we simply legislated it.

Wouldn't be great if we could legislate that our meetings be spiritual and nurturing? That Friends arrive to worship on time? That worship be inspiring, and coming to meeting be fun? But we can't legislate meeting. We can only fix what is "normal" through collective example.

AMONG FAVORITES

If Quakerism is experiential, as we claim, how can we present it in a way that novices understand? I pondered this question as I prepared to speak about vocal ministry in the orientation class I was leading. I figured I would tell *my* own favorites. I chose the most significant ones:

The most *profound* one shed light on the spiritual nature of meeting. By virtue of our worshipful presence, it said, we create a sacred space that invites the emergence of the divine Spirit. I had often felt that irresistible power forcing me to get up and speak.

The most *inspiring* one captured all that had happened in meeting in twenty years. The speaker, a long-absent young Friend, had blossomed into a confident, charismatic, and spiritual adult. On that Easter Sunday, I heard the most eloquent and uplifting message ever.

One Friend gave praise for being big enough to connect with the largest in the Universe and small enough to relate to the smallest. I reckoned he was wrong on both counts, but I still think of his words long after he has forgotten them. It has become my most *intriguing* message.

A young man with Down syndrome was among our mentally-challenged visitors one day. His emotional and well-spoken words became my most *memorable* message. He proved that the Spirit knows no limits.

Impartial as I may be, the most *adorable* message was the one our five-year-old granddaughter spoke at her aunt's wedding ceremony. Moved by a spontaneous Spirit, she delivered a concise, well-thought-out, and thematic speech that left in awe Friends and friends alike.

SEE IT WITH THE LIGHT

For an upcoming program, Friends were asked to consider favorite verses from Bible Class. The lure to find rest for my soul was an enticing candidate. So was the mysterious sin against the Holy Spirit, along with the enigmatic command to love your enemy and to bless the one who hates you.

The verse that I have chosen gives praise for the hidden things the wise can't see but have been revealed to the innocent. Plain, simple-minded folks came to the surface; peasants in my ancestral village, for instance, whose lives centered on livestock and crops, but in their grasp of the world, they matched the best of the pundits around.

I reflected on the Bedouin with whom I had the privilege to spend time. Their lives are like a continuous meeting for worship under the desert sky. In fact, most stars as known today had been named by their ancestors—the ancient nomads of Arabia. The Bedouin have gained world understanding and full control of their domain through self-reliance and the power of their Inner Light.

And then I thought of the Pharisees who have mastered the appearance of the sky but couldn't fathom the signs of the times. In their scholarship and obsession with the law, they lost touch with reality. The simple things the innocent could see were hidden from them.

Seeing the hidden spoke the most to my condition. It reaffirmed the advantage of simplicity, the benefits of seasoning, and the blessings of spiritual discernment. The provocative verse brings home the simple truth: There *is* no substitute for the Inner Light.

A WORD ABOUT THE ROBE

The king holds a feast for his son's wedding. He invites many, but few come. Some go to their fields, others to their stores. These guests are unworthy, declares the king, and sends servants to bring in anyone they find on the street.

The king's guests are his close subjects. At the time of the banquet, they have other matters to attend to, as many of the sons and daughters of meeting do. The king is not happy, but he understands. He gets upset only when a guest comes to the banquet without his wedding robe.

The king wants to hold the banquet, and so he finds new guests. Meetings are full of new Friends. They are vital to the viability of Quakerism.

The king finds new guests for he has a party. There must be a party for guests to come, and it must be a good one, for many parties go on around town. But when seekers leave half way through worship, I must ask: Do *we* have one?

The crux of the story, though, is the robe of contention.

Clearly, the folks on the street had no wedding robes. The king's ire is aimed only at the guest who did not wear the robe he had been given.

As vital as the robe is to the banquet, so is the grasp of Quaker basics to the life of meeting. Seekers don't come with it. It must be provided by meeting.

How can seekers wear a robe they don't have?

What if they won't wear the robe they were given?

IN THE BEGINNING

In the beginning God created heaven and earth. The earth was dark and without form. According to the biblical tale, God said let there be light, and there was light. God then carried out some major firmament and water-collection works we couldn't possibly understand.

Soon there were fruit trees, and grass, and creeping creatures feeding on them. Having created man, by the end of the sixth day, God's work was done. And so, on the seventh day, God laid back to admire His Creation. God saw that everything He had made was very good.

The legend of Creation and God's rest on the seventh day gave rise to the tradition of the Sabbath. For six days, men must work to carry out their respective parts in making the world go around as we know it. The Sabbath is the chance to get off the treadmill and regain perspective.

Today we have not one but two Sabbath days. They open the door to pursuits beyond duty—creative expression, new learning, or simple play. Regrettably, Sabbath reflection has morphed into amusement aimed at taking our minds off work. With that, we not only cloud our perspective, but we devalue our accomplishments.

Worship, for a brief moment each week, is the chance to leave our treadmill behind. Besides counting all the blessings bestowed upon us, we may reflect on our work, our successes, and the challenges we have overcome.

God wasn't shy in Creation. He looked upon all parts of His work with pride, joy, and satisfaction. Whether our work has been filled with satisfaction or drudgery, we can follow God's example, for all *we* have done is very good.

IMAGINE

In my high school days of yore, math mysteries fascinated me as much as the mysteries of the Spirit do today. "i," the square root of minus one, had special hold. It wasn't the shock of an imaginary number but the imaginary world that sprouted around it. Without much fanfare, a bizarre parallel "math life" came into being.

Two things brought this recently to mind. The first was the ubiquitous Alt-key on the keyboard. I came to realize that by holding it down, the good-old numbers pad that I used for decades to crunch numbers for a living can take me into an imaginary world. As if by magic, I can now create my own hearts, and music notes, and smiley faces.

In turn, the Parable of the Vineyard presents another world as well—the parallel universe of the Spirit. There *are* owners, and vineyards, and workers in that world, but the rules, the logic, and the rewards that apply are not the ones we know from our ordinary lives.

The Alt-key is an either-or proposition. You may have numbers *or* symbols but not both. Mixing them is not possible. You know what world you are in at all times. But as we navigate the spiritual world, challenges become evident. Reality seems to intersect the two. We do live in a world of rules and figures, but applying ordinary math to love, compassion, or ministry is futile.

Try to prove the presence of the Spirit to a neophyte. How strong are the promptings of the Spirit? Try putting a figure on the impact of the Light on people or on the size of the blessings that may come from doing good works. I now miss the world of "i." I pine for imaginary formulae to illuminate my new imaginary world.

A LESSON FROM CITY HALL

Boston, Massachusetts, receives twelve million tourists a year. I learned that while spending a few days there on a mini vacation. A plethora of guided tours cater to the crowd's thirst for knowledge. The focus of the tours is the momentous history of the city, at the center of which is the gold-domed Old State House.

In its many lives, the modest two-story building has served the State legislature, housed City Hall, and at inception, was Boston's first public building. Those were stormy days. Within its walls, heated debate and fateful decisions led to the American Revolution. Thousands of lives were affected. Thousands of lives were lost.

Nowadays, the building is silent. No musket-wielding patriots roam the streets, no British ships patrol the harbor, and there are no explosions coming from Bunker Hill. Only the mobs of tourists mill aimlessly around the aging structure.

Next to it is Boston's new financial district. The multi-colored skyscrapers that engulf the golden globe define the city. The cries of the revolution have been supplanted by modern chatter from high above. The historical tumult has been erased by a new reality. It has been transcended.

I came to realize that transcendence is the best remedy for the ills of the past. It is the best way to overcome trauma, failure, and darkness. Memories and feelings cannot be erased. They *can* be transcended.

Boston's iconic postcard with its urban-jungle-flanked colonial midget is now securely pinned onto my wall. Transcendence is my new spiritual assignment.

WHY COME TO MEETING?

Psalms casts unexpected light onto this weighty question.

> Blessed is the man on the path of the Spirit
> Like a tree planted by streams of water
> Fruit in season will bear; its leaf will not wither

A man in the Light is like a robust tree that withstands the elements and yields everlasting fruit. The Light is the anchor of a successful life. Without it, man will flounder and like chaff in the wind is blown away.

Broadchurch—the British TV show—is a good example. It is the story of ordinary people living ordinary lives in an ordinary town. Absorbed by their routines, they slowly lose their spiritual grounding. Without the anchor of life-sustaining Light, they slide into an abyss of no return.

As tragedy follows tragedy, it becomes clear that without its moral compass, the town is no longer a community. From the deep bottom, the town pulls together again. Its citizens find redemption in a renewed community, galvanized by the Light of spiritual awakening.

*   *

Friends come to meeting to find spiritual grounding. An outsider is likely to say that sitting hours on end doing nothing is a strange way of showing it.

But when Friends gather in worship—all of the same mind, settled in the divine Light, and centered on the dearest to their hearts—something tangible happens.

With nurture from each other and guidance from the Light, we create the spiritual anchor that puts us onto the path of life and draws us back to meeting week after week.

TELL ME ABOUT QUAKERS

In three plain words, Quakers, slash Friends, are peaceful, truthful, and simple.

On the first Sunday after the summer doldrums, our meeting house was packed. A Friend stood up and said: It's so nice to see all of us gathered together as Friends. On that sunny day, Friends could have been in many places, but they chose to come to worship in meeting.

Worship, in so many ways, is what is dearest to one's heart. Friends bring their worshipful presence to meeting and, together, create a sacred spiritual space. It is the silence of that space that invites the emergence of the Spirit and the guidance of the Light.

In that safe spiritual oasis and with the insights of others, we seek to get closer to the Light and to find answers to the kind of persons we are called to be and how to proceed with our lives. As result, we are often led to take a stand on matters regarding peace, social justice, and stewardship of the Earth.

In worship, we may give praise for the good in our lives or connect with the good in all people. We may rejoice in the glory of God's Creation or steer challenges in our lives toward the Light. The silence may inspire a message from a Friend. That message may speak to our condition, for worship is a time of insight, revelation, and healing.

Worship does not end at the front door. Friends, like honey-bees darting from flower to flower, seek the truth everywhere they go. A "spiritual beehive" may be the best metaphor for meeting, for on First Days, Friends return to it to share in worship their spiritual nectar.

THE VOICE OF THE SPIRIT...OR MINE?

A Quaker Orientation Class is currently in progress at my meeting. The class is unique in the sense that no previous knowledge is required, there is no need to read anything, and there is no homework. It is a hands-on class, one might say. The only assignment is to be in the Spirit.

What it means is that for the six-week duration of the class, everyone must carry the Spirit of the class everywhere they go. Everybody must be on constant lookout for how that Spirit affects their actions, decisions, and interaction with others. The "everybody" includes the leader. And that would be me.

So, here I am, duly thinking about the class. I am thinking about the up-coming session on vocal ministry. I will tell the class that Friends center to clear their hearts and minds of all thoughts, so the thoughts from the Spirit may come in. Then, they will ask how do we know which ones are ours and which are from the Spirit.

I have thought about that for a long time.

I don't yet have a stellar answer, but I do have a rule of thumb: If the thought is boring it's mine. If it is novel, it comes out of the blue without reason, and it won't let up, it is from the Spirit. If I am debating myself about some long-unresolved matter, it is mine. As such, ordinarily, I wouldn't be moved to share this thought today.

On the other hand, thoughts evoked by other Friends vocal ministry can only be spirit-led. And so, just as I began to realize that my boring self-debate about a seemingly insolvable matter was not letting up, our Friend wondered what others may be thinking in worship today.

IS THE KINGDOM IN OR OUT?

Paul, the last remnant of Friends once Christ-centered way of life, would be one hundred-years old today. Paul took that approach seriously and was often out of sync with the new realities in meeting. But Paul and I had something in common. We both sat in our own spots in worship, and so, for almost two decades, Paul and I shook hands at the rise of every meeting.

"The Kingdom of Heaven on Earth" was Paul's favorite saying, and he found creative ways to plug it into his speech. Paul's mind was sharp, but he was well past his prime, and his decreased mobility restricted his social interactions to his seat. I took advantage of that condition to probe Paul about what lay behind his favorite quote.

The Kingdom of Heaven may have dire connotations to some Friends. To me, hearing it for the first time, the Kingdom of Heaven carried a mysterious ring—if not a prophetic one then a medieval one at least. But Paul and I were too far apart in our thinking, and whatever he may have said about it went right over my head.

Today, many years later and after four years of Friendly Bible study, the answer is fairly evident to me. Jesus taught simple things to simple people. The Kingdom of Heaven on Earth—the essence of his ministry—simply states that by working together we can create a world of harmony and abundance for all mankind.

Friends may still have qualms with the implications of the somewhat anachronistic term. But aren't the Quaker testimonies meant to accomplish just that—a peaceful, sustainable, and just world where we all live a life of purpose and spiritual fulfilment?

ZACCHAEUS MAKES IT SIMPLE

The key to solving math problems is precise definition of variables. In the realm of the Spirit, however, definitions are elusive. Therefore, to gain clearness, I look at bewildering matters from more than just one angle. Take the unforgivable sin.

Jesus says all sins are forgiven, except one—the sin against the Holy Spirit. Here, as in math, a precise definition of sin, forgiveness, and the Holy Spirit would be handy. As those are hard to come by, I ask in reverse: What is the only thing that cannot ever be undone? That is life itself.

The unforgivable sin is against life—the Light within each and every human being. It is the sin against the special God-given gifts and talents that make each of us one of a kind. If you wasted them, you wasted the only life you had. No remedy can turn back the clock.

*　　*

As the biblical Zacchaeus miraculously repents, Jesus says life has come to his house. Zacchaeus, too mired in his tax-collecting duties, failed to see the misery his actions had brought to his fellow men. By making amends, he makes a contribution to the Kingdom. It brings him eternal life.

The Kingdom of Heaven is a world where all men work together living in harmony and abundance. By applying one's God-given gifts to building a peaceful, sustainable, and spiritually fulfilling future, one becomes part of it.

Entering the Kingdom means eternal life

All else is a waste of the God-given gifts

ALL OR NOTHING

No matter who you are or where you came from, once you enter its doors, London's Westminster Abbey will make your jaw drop in awe. Regardless of the history and the politics behind its existence, the splendor inside is the epitome of the human spirit. It is the best money can buy.

People in all civilizations have built glorious monuments to what they held dearest to their hearts. In a way, Europe's cathedrals seem to have one purpose only—to defy the laws of gravity and the limits of architecture. The best minds of each generation created the ultimate sensory perfection for the worship of God.

Friends meeting houses, on the other hand, are simple outside and plain inside. There are no ornaments on the windows, no paintings on the walls. No statues of saints line the aisles. Friends have simply decided that the worship of God is inside—in the hearts of the people.

Just as modern art gave up perfectionism in favor of capturing essence, Friends search for the essence of the Spirit is a natural evolution. But by placing God in the hearts of men, Friends made the task much more difficult.

In this scheme, every person is a cathedral full of heavenly color and sound—a monument worthy of divine worship; God's unique recreation of the whole world.

It's an all or nothing proposition.

If we are true to that ideal, if we live up to the worship of the Inner Light, we have it all—cathedrals, ornaments and a thriving Spirit. Otherwise, we have nothing but white walls and emptiness inside.

QUAKERISM IS ALL THAT

Hygge, the Danish togetherness, is a mental state induced by candlelight on dark winter nights and the company of family and friends. The German Gemütlichkeit is not only cheerful, congenial comfort, but also an unhurried peace of mind and a sense of belonging and acceptance.

Wabi-sabi is the love for what already is. It's the Japanese acceptance of the tolls of life and worn-out imperfections. It means less waste and more mindfulness. It works well with kaizen—the principle of continuous betterment. Jugaad, in turn, is India's reverence for innovative fixes.

Lastly, friluftsliv is Norwegian for fresh air life. Like the Japanese shinrin-yoku—the literal forest bathing—it is about the power of the outdoors to heal mind and spirit.

These are inspiring concepts employed by people around the world but, allegedly, are absent from the American culture. The essayist must have overlooked Quakerism.

I find pronounced togetherness when Friends of one mind settle in peaceful, unhurried worship, centered on what is dearest to their hearts. Breaking bread with Friends is welcoming and congenial and offers the Gemütlichkeit sense of belonging and social acceptance.

Simplicity, continuing revelation and stewardship are testimonies of reverence for the old, hope for a better future, and prudence about nature's treasures.

By saying that the Light resides in the hearts of men, Fox took worship away from the steeple, into the open. Our annual outdoor worship meeting is the cherished event of the year, filling mind and spirit with air and sunshine.

I SHINE MY LIGHT FOR OTHERS TO LOVE

It's midnight. The captain, on the bridge of the ship for final inspection, sees a bright object straight ahead. He signals right away: "You are on collision course. Move ten east; over." The response is immediate: "You are on collision course. Move ten west; over."

The captain is in no mood for jokes. "I am Captain Jones," he says "move ten east; over." "I am Attendant Matthews. Move ten west; over." The captain is furious. "I am a destroyer with five thousand sailors onboard," he barks, "I'm not moving!" "I am the Lighthouse with one part-time help; your choice."

The captain may simply be an arrogant snob. But with his focus on himself, the captain lost his sense of relevance. Alas, the lighthouse keeper does the same. While both are right in a way, no one would argue that running a destroyer into a lighthouse is a smart thing to do.

In the words of early Friends, both put form over substance. Who they are and what they say does not change the truth. Jesus, too, speaks a great deal about the often elusive principle of placing spirit over letter.

But the hero in this anecdote is the lighthouse.

Shining its light is its only purpose. It shines it for all the ships, all the time. It shines it evenly to best serve all captains in the darkness, no matter what they may say.

In a culture as ours, based on incentives and positive reinforcement, the lighthouse is the perfect role model; a role model that single-mindedly and unconditionally, shines its light for others to love—the best it knows how.

THAT LIGHT OF MINE—TAKE TWO

It's midnight. The captain of the ship is on the bridge for final inspection when he sees a bright object straight ahead. He signals right away: "You are on collision course. Move ten east; over." The response is immediate: "You are on collision course. Move ten west; over."

The captain is in no mood for jokes. "I am Captain Jones," he says "move ten east; over." "I am Attendant Matthews. Move ten west; over." The captain is furious. "I am a destroyer with five thousand sailors onboard," he barks, "I'm not moving!" "I am the Lighthouse with one part-time helper; your choice."

One may simply dismiss the captain as an arrogant snob who lost his good sense of relevance. The hero in this anecdote, though, is the lighthouse. Shining its light is its sole purpose. It shines its light unconditionally to best serve the captains of all the ships all the time.

The Kingdom of Heaven, Jesus says, is like the owner of the vineyard who hires workers throughout the day. When they all get paid equally, the workers who toiled all day complain about fairness. The parable suggests that working for the Kingdom is without preconditions.

As such, the lighthouse is the perfect role model. It is true to its purpose regardless of how many ships happen to go by, whether the captains like its light or not, or what they may or may not say about it.

Be it a leading we may pursue or simply doing what is right ordered, the lighthouse is a reminder not to ever worry about numbers, not to ever seek validation in results.

THAT LIGHT OF MINE—TAKE THREE

It must be harvest time in the vineyard, for the owner hires anyone he can possibly find. Some get to work in the morning, others at noon, and some in the afternoon. At the end of the day, when the owner pays them the same, those who toiled all day complain about fairness.

Many lessons emerge from the passage, but above all, there is a practical truth: work for the Kingdom is without preconditions. To Friends, that translates into the pursuit of a leading or the taking of an action simply for being right ordered.

No one expressed that better than Bob—the living force behind the men's group in meeting. One night when only the two of us came, Bob gave me a smile and said: "I'm here every Friday no matter how many Friends come. At times, I am here by myself."

Those words of wisdom resurfaced as we celebrated Emily's life. Emily was a long-time member of our meeting, with family connections spanning three and four generations. Friends and friends reiterated the many ways in which Emily had shaped their spiritual life.

Memorial services are busy, and so I said nothing. I didn't know Emily well, but for that very reason, in the context of the spiritual life of meeting, my message may have been equally important.

Emily's presence in meeting extended well beyond her close friends. I, too, registered her unassuming ways, her peculiar ministry, and the strength of her spirit. Emily didn't worry about numbers. Her mantra was simple: Just do it! And she did.

WHY STILL A QUAKER?

Along my spiritual journey, I have learned life-changing lessons. Valuable as they may be, they are in the past. I could write a thank you note to the meeting clerk and simply move on. Why am I still a Quaker *now*?

In the wake of such enormous personal transformation, one may remain a Quaker for life out of gratitude alone. But spiritual metamorphosis comes from work. Transformation is the result of things we do. So what do Quakers do?

*   *

My top-ten Quaker To-Dos

10-Receive guidance and nurture via worship and Friends

9-Continue my revelation for meaning and purpose

8-Perfect my knowledge about the Inner Light

7-Perfect my knowledge about my place in the Universe

6-Perfect my principled life and my "right thing to do"

5-Gain spiritual empowerment and spiritual authority

4-Bear witness through my actions and deeds

3-Seek the truth everywhere and speak the truth always

2-Shine my Light for others to love

Above all
Minister to lift the spiritual life and well-being of others

180

Other

Downingtown Friends Meeting house est. 1806
Chester County, Pennsylvania

The Downingtown Friends Meeting house is a Quaker
house of worship built in 1806.

In 2006, as Friends celebrated the Meeting bicentennial,
the two-century-old building receiving a full facelift.

Downingtown Friends Meeting has a two-hundred-strong
membership.

It provides a supportive environment for spiritual growth
and a loving, nurturing, and happy place for the children of
the community.

Downingtown Friends Meeting
Bicentennial Tree Dedication
Downingtown, Pennsylvania, 2006

The pin oak sapling planted on that day honors two centuries of Friends presence in the community.

The sapling symbolizes the vitality of our Quaker community and the hope for the two hundred years to come.

In the years since, the pin oak has steadily grown and now it is visible from inside the meeting house.

Metaphorically, it reminds us over and again that spiritual growth and transformation are slow, steady processes.

With nurture and patience, the spirit becomes stronger and more in tune with the Divine—all the time.

OF SPIRITUAL ENDOWMENT

About the time of our bicentennial, Worship and Ministry saw it right ordered that Friends serving on the committee should take turns sitting on the facing benches. The sense of the committee was that it created continuity.

As most Friends do, I prefer my regular seat in meeting and found myself somewhat disjointed being above the others in the room. I soon realized, however, that I was more unsettled by what lay behind me than in front of me—the hundreds of Friends buried in the field outside the window.

I felt their presence as if another meeting for worship were in progress out there high up above the cemetery. No doubt, meeting meant a great deal to their spiritual lives. It was their anchor as they struggled and overcame hardships. Meeting sustained their ideals, visions, and aspirations. In their lives, they followed principles and convictions.

Their presence paved the way to the future and enabled us to enjoy our spiritual home. Centuries of their worship added substance and gravity to the stone building. It became clear to me that without the people, the sparkling building was just that—not a house of worship but just another ancient stone structure.

Other than a few recurring names on the graves like Parke, Downing, and Thomas, I know nothing about them. Even though their spiritual endowment would have been invaluable, all they have left behind are a few mysterious carvings in the wooden benches of the meeting house. I didn't know those Friends.

But these Friends I did know:

Sixteen Teachers

Charlie

Charlie walked in the Light
in his own way of amused levity

Seemingly above the fray of everyday life
he cheerfully balanced self-deprecation
with irresistible dark humor

Charlie always left you in an improved frame of mind

He was always surrounded by Friends
curious to hear what Charlie would say next

Charlie earned his well-deserved spot on
"Milton—the Happy Rock"
as a Friend who walked through life with a smile

Bob

DuPont scientist turned Quaker
Bob epitomized Friends goodness and peacefulness

Bob was the guiding light of DFM men's group

Bob knew that leadings of the Spirit
aren't driven by results but by the desire to minister
One must act when action is right

I'm here whether ten Friends come or none
Bob once said of the group

Bob saw the fallacy in judging ministry by end results

For who will be touched by the Spirit and how
resides in the domain of eternal mystery

Paul

Paul's devotion to Downingtown Friends was unshakable
A life-long Friend, Paul made great efforts to attend
meeting even as his health was in grave decline

Paul's personal integrity was beyond reproach
His humility and unwavering spiritual integrity
shone like beacons of Light

Paul was the last remnant of Friends
once Christ-centered way of life
With his departure, that link has been lost

I wish I had the vision and fortitude to probe more
That lost opportunity is a reminder that
hiding under the bushel comes in many shades

The Kingdom of Heaven was Paul's favorite phrase

Paul must be smiling today as we at DFM are
miraculously engaged in studying the teachings of Jesus

191

Virginia

Virginia was one of the white-haired
heavenly-smile women at Downingtown Meeting

New Friends in meeting
perplexed by the mystical inner workings of Quakerism
looked to Virginia as the one who had seen the Light,
the one who held all the answers inside her vest

Virginia walked cheerfully in the Light
answering that of God in everyone
Her energy permeated her surroundings and
touched each and every person around her

For decades, Virginia was a
Quaker ambassador to the community and a
Friendly presence in Downingtown Friends Meeting

Ellis

Ellis Brown, III became a member of DFM in...1912
Ellis sat in colorful outfits on the facing bench
surveying Friends in worship with big blue eyes
He never once uttered a word

A jolting stir swept the room one day as
Ellis slowly rose and said in deep, well-paced voice
This may be the time to take up
the business of the monthly meeting

I cornered Ellis one day and asked him point blank
Ellis, what do you think about in meeting?
Good things, I hope, he blurted cryptically

Through his steadfast ways
Ellis defined the essence of Friends worship
A life-long, unconditional practice
of private communion with the Divine

John

John is a hero for his principles and his resolve
Above all
John is a hero for his courage to stand in harm's way
for those principles no matter what

John followed the leadings of the Spirit
beyond the zone of comfort
He showed us that roadblocks cannot dim our vision
nor can setbacks snag our drive

The adage
Build a solid foundation with the bricks life throws at you
applies to John more than anyone I know
John eagerly awaited those bricks
He applied them to strengthen his resolve

Marie

"Marie Waldron Inslee, 88, was a Quaker schoolteacher
who fought for environmental and social causes
She once offered to write a personal check
to help a would-be robber straighten his life out"
That is how Marie was memorialized
by the Philadelphia Inquirer

Her waist-long white hair made Marie look like an angel
Her voice was so faint that only the nearest Friends
could enjoy her ministry and chuckle at times
But her spirit shone and eyes were full of life
Marie bequeathed that indomitable spirit to us

Marie once opined: Why don't Friends speak in meeting?
They must be thinking something
It was an empowering statement

Marie symbolizes an intrepid life
Never give up
Never give up

Clarita & Paul

Clarita—Reat
Reat was one of our three white-haired ladies
Her presence brought Light and inspiration to meeting
Through her compassion and empathy
Reat defined the essence of the peaceful Quaker

Paul
I am waiting for Paul to suddenly appear in meeting
It feels as if Paul's never-ending smile
is still hovering above us

Paul lovingly shared his artistic talents
He proved that ministry can touch people in unique ways
That was especially true with children

As we approached Paul stretched on his lounge chair
our toddler promptly jumped onto him and
proceeded to pick his white beard
Politely, Paul protested my embarrassment by saying
that he enjoyed it. But then he added: immensely

Francis

Francis loved retelling his father's words of concern:
"Downingtown Meeting may die out"
It didn't and Francis may be the reason why

Francis availed spiritual guidance to Friends for decades
making Downingtown Friends a rich spiritual home

A spiritually strong meeting is a strong meeting, he said It
was Francis's marching order for Friends:
Figure out what that is and make it happen

His tenacity had lasting effect all around him
be it the Philadelphia Peace Conference or
the revival of the century-long dormant Caln Meeting
When Francis put his mind to it, nothing could stop him

Above all, Francis had unparalleled spiritual authority
both admirable and enviable
It has been Francis's greatest gift to Friends

Lou

With a full head of grey hair and piercing eyes
eighty-year-old Lou was clearly a weighty Friend
Silent expectation often meant waiting for Lou to rise and
deliver yet another eloquent, mind-provoking message

Lou became a Quaker for the peace testimony
To him, moral principles meant nothing
unless applied to the human condition
With that in mind, Lou began his four-decade
service with AFSC, retiring as General Secretary

Lou was among those on the ground who earned Friends
Nobel Peace Prize. His work of unbiased service and
reconciliation went on as he guided AFSC through the
turbulent years of Civil Rights and the Vietnam War

Lou's intrepid spirit echoed in meeting
He spoke his mind no matter how unwanted his view was
A meeting at Lou's turned into an emotional outpouring
I feel I am at my own memorial service, Lou said.
And he was

Keitha

After a thirty-year sojourn at Downingtown Friends,
Keitha and Doug retired to their home meeting

Keitha has worn so many hats in meeting
It simply didn't seem possible that
Downingtown Friends could function without her

Through her powerful witness in the Light
Keitha always knew the right thing to do

That is far from being a simple matter
Friends often wrestle with discernment of authority
and gaining support for personal leadings

Keitha's take on Quaker authority was a pragmatic one
Alex, she said to me once
If you want to do something just go ahead and do it
until somebody stops you

I am still working on that

Doug

From the very first sight
Doug's demeanor projected a "very important" person
Doug wasn't nominated or appointed by anyone
His "authority" came solely from his Inner Light

Doug wove levity into his spiritual life in enigmatic ways
His vocal ministry was weighty, yet distinctly anecdotal
What's more important, Doug once asked in earnest,
peace or justice? You can't have both

Doug visited me as I mourned losses in my garden
He looked around and quickly said
Do you have successes out there?
His question was a life-changing proposition

What's done is done
At some point any garden will suffer damage
Keeping score just makes no sense
Seeking successes, though, is looking into the future
Their anticipation is a gift of continuing revelation

Hugh

Hugh had only been a short time at Downingtown Friends
but he left his mark on meeting and Friends

Hugh was an ordained minister and
an active pastor for close to three decades

Deep in his heart Hugh was a Quaker
He was drawn to the mysticism of silence
and attended meeting in tandem with his ministry
Upon retirement, Hugh became a bona fide Friend

Hugh's humility and God's love in his heart
preceded him throughout

Hugh never let his professional credentials
affect his interactions in meeting

His consent to lead a Bible study group
was delayed by that concern until a Quaker way opened

Dean

Had anyone kept count of messages over
his four decades in meeting, Dean would have
outnumbered all other Friends combined

As a norm, Dean's messages bubbled up five minutes
before the rise of meeting, creating a welcomed
anticipation—silent expectation at its best

Dean's vocal ministry came from his life-long experience
of teaching Biology and his continuous ponderings about
the mysteries of God's Creation

My right size in the Universe, once Dean said
Allows me to comprehend the largest of galaxies
and the tiniest of quarks
I thought he was wrong on both counts

But what Dean has probably forgotten I haven't

I think of it every day

Gerry

Gerry's jovial portrait evokes a good-natured
happy go lucky, oversized teddy bear—which he is
But to someone who has known Gerry for a long time
the Rock of Gibraltar is a far better analogy

Gerry's stature and booming voice
mesmerize people around him
When Gerry speaks, people listen

Gerry proudly traces his lineage to the earliest Friends
and keeps their heritage alive
Moreover, Gerry epitomizes Friends ideal of
seeking the truth and speaking the truth

Gerry wears his Quakerism on his sleeve
He carries out his testimonies as a way of life
Be it a friend in trouble, meeting short a hand,
or neighbors in need of help
Gerry, the Good Samaritan, is there
like the Rock—solid, dependent, resourceful

Judith

By the time of my arrival
Judith had been in meeting for a long-time

In their own way, Judith and her husband Bob
were very active in meeting and to me
very much a part of it

Judith was one of the frequent speakers
in meeting for worship
Her messages were about everyday life
Her vocal ministry proved that spirituality is everywhere

I looked forward to Judith speaking
Her messages were colorful and anecdotal
At times, they felt a bit off-center even to a neophyte
But Judith spoke as moved by the Spirit

Honoring the Spirit was Judith's greatest gift to Friends

Quaker
Miscellanea

QUAKER LINGO

Centering—the practice at the start of worship of clearing the mind and the heart of all external thoughts

Clearness—the opening to the leadings of the Spirit, especially in ambiguous situations

Continuing Revelation—the belief that the Spirit of God has not ceased to speak to people even today

Discernment—the search for the truth in trying situations

Hold in the Light—recognize concern for another person's condition

Inner Light—the universal life force. Also called the Inner Teacher, the Christ within, the Light of God or the Holy Spirit to denote its divine nature and infinite power

Leading—a course of action, belief, or conviction that a Friend feels is divinely inspired

Meeting for Worship—a weekly meeting where Friends worship in silent expectation

Silent Expectation—a description of Quaker worship where Friends sit in silence expecting the divine Spirit

Testimonies—*the* Quaker beliefs based in action geared toward peace, social justice, and Earth stewardship

That of God in Everyone—the belief that the presence of God is within all people

Vocal Ministry—the act of speaking during worship

QUAKER BELIEFS

For over 350 years, Friends have sought the guidance of the Inner Light to the truth. Today, Friends meetings offer a safe spiritual oasis to continue the inward search. In the spirit of the teachings of Jesus and the nurture of others, we seek answers to the kind of persons we are called to be and how to proceed in our lives.

As a result of that introspection and the belief of the Light of God in everyone, Friends are often led to take a stand on matters related to peace, social justice, and the stewardship of the Earth.

"The Light of God is in everyone" is the logical conclusion of God's creating all men in His image. It is often extended to include Earth and its creatures, making all God's Creation divine. It is the foundation of Friends main testimonies. That of God in everyone explains Friends reverence for the sanctity of life.

Ministry to others is a universal aptitude and human need. Friends are all ministers, responsible for the spiritual well-being of the self and the community. To Friends, every encounter may carry a message. Every person can be a teacher, and every detail of God's Creation a sacrament.

Friends trust the continuing of divine revelation to inspire them and to bring meaning into their lives. A life of simplicity sustains one's spiritual channels to God, open and unencumbered by that which is nonessential.

Simplicity is a matter of keeping our material surroundings directly serviceable to necessary ends. Simplicity patterns thought and speech—true, plain, and direct. Simplicity supports the humility and the integrity of the Spirit.

QUAKER SPIRITUALITY

Spirituality is a process of examination. The outward look probes the big picture of the Universe and our place in it. The meaning and purpose of life, the nature of God and soul, and our union with the Divine are common themes in the metaphysical search.

The inward look examines matters of ethics as they affect the self. We seek answers to the kind of persons we are and the kind we are called to become. We seek the guidance of the Spirit to discern the divine calling for our lives.

Spirituality grows our vision, wisdom, and fortitude. It propels us to live a principled life where actions are not driven by needs and desires but by that which is right.

SPIRITUAL ESSENTIALS

ENLIGHTENMENT—a state in one's spiritual journey rich in lessons learned and truths found

GOD—the primal catalytic force embodied in the Universe

MINISTRY—attendance to the spiritual needs of others

PRESENCE OF THE DIVINE—worshipful reverence to the infinite powers of the Universe

SALVATION—redemption from a meaningless life

SPIRIT—the spiritual force within that tells me what to do

WISDOM—the power of discerning what is true and right

WORSHIP—ardent devotion to the dearest to one's heart

ONE QUAKER'S FAVORITE QUOTES

- You may be only one person in the world
  but you may be the world to one person
- When everything is coming at you, you are in the
  wrong lane
- If you worry about what others say
  you lose sight of what you want
- An un-laughed life is not worth living
- The Kingdom of Heaven will only arrive
  if people will live their lives as if it has
- Let us see what love can do
- All which doesn't make you alive is too small for you
- A silver lining is in every cloud; my job is to find it
- War does not decide who is right—only who is left
- All things needed for your calling will come to you at
  the right time; stop interfering in your own life
- Some look for beautiful places. Others make them
- One day your life will flash before your eyes
  Make sure it will be worth watching
- The Light lurks in everyone; one just needs to get it out
- Find what you love. Love what you find
- Are you good at math? Count your blessings
- Make the most of all that comes, least of all that goes
- Be yourself! Everyone else is taken
- The greatest truths are found in the darkest hours
- No problem can be solved with the brain that created it
- Let us reach for the world that ought to be
- Belief in what is desirable rarely suffices to achieve it
- We don't see things the way they are
  We see them the way *we* are
- When you do good, good is more likely to happen
- Lay a sound foundation with the bricks thrown at you
- Wherever you go, whatever the weather
  always bring your own sunshine with you
- All things come into your life to bring you to the
  ultimate realization of who you are
- Close your eyes, look inside; fantasy will set you free